THE
COLOURS
OF MY
HEART

THE
COLOURS
OF MY
HEART

selected
poems

FAIZ AHMED FAIZ

Translated from the Urdu by
Baran Farooqi

PENGUIN BOOKS
An imprint of Penguin Random House

PENGUIN BOOKS

USA | Canada | UK | Ireland | Australia
New Zealand | India | South Africa | China | Singapore

Penguin Books is part of the Penguin Random House group of companies
whose addresses can be found at global.penguinrandomhouse.com

Published by Penguin Random House India Pvt. Ltd
4th Floor, Capital Tower 1, MG Road,
Gurugram 122 002, Haryana, India

First published in Penguin Books by Penguin Random House India 2017

10 9 8 7 6

ISBN 9780670086054

Typeset in Adobe Caslon Pro by Manipal Digital Systems, Manipal
Printed at Replika Press Pvt. Ltd, India

www.penguin.co.in

This is a legitimate digitally printed version of the book and therefore might not
have certain extra finishing on the cover.

Contents

Contents

Contents

Contents

Zindaan Nama

Contents

Contents

Contents

Shaam-e Shahr-e Yaaraan

Contents

Contents

Translator's Introduction

Faiz Ahmed Faiz was born in 1911 in Kala Qadir, a village near Sialkot, now in Pakistan. He died in November 1984, having lived an illustrious life as the leading Urdu poet of his time. He was the one modern Urdu poet after Iqbal whose fame and reputation spread far beyond the boundaries of language and place. He was a poet whom the world knew for his melodious poetic voice and revolutionary message—a message, it must be added, that was never delivered in a strident or rabble-rousing manner. His poetry continues to charm and fascinate generations of poets and readers after him. In fact, eminent writers of the 1960s, who professed to scoff at the achievements of the Progressives, spared and stinted nothing in admiring Faiz and writing about him.

It is clear that Faiz became a legend in his lifetime. Many factors contributed to the Faiz phenomenon: his image as a revolutionary who had an aristocratic background; the circumstances of his political life (he was imprisoned twice for his political acts and beliefs and went into self-exile later); his personal charm and his refusal to be dragged into controversies or even reply to his critics (of whom there were many to begin with, especially in the so-called 'classical' camp); the music of his verse and its rich imagery which was not only evocative of Urdu poetry's resplendent and much-admired premodern idiom, but which also still sounded contemporary and relevant; and his melancholy voice which was never devoid of undertones of hope and promise. As his reputation grew, so did his image, so much so that it almost became larger than life. And its lustre continues to dazzle us long after his death in 1984.

The Making of a Poet

Faiz was born in incredibly turbulent times for the world at large, and particularly for the Indian subcontinent. Though born into an affluent, aristocratic family (his grandfather had been a provincial governor in Afghanistan), Faiz did not go abroad to study like some of his peers from wealthy families. He studied philosophy and English literature in

Lahore and finished with an MA in Arabic. He started his career as a junior lecturer in a college at Amritsar. What was it like to be Faiz Ahmed in those times (for Faiz hadn't yet adopted for himself the pen name Faiz Ahmed Faiz)?

It was 1934–35. Anti-British, or nationalistic sentiment, the desire for freedom, to rid the country of the foreigner, was everywhere in the air. So was, unfortunately, the feeling of 'communal' conflict between the two main communities of Hindus and Muslims. Left-wing thought was making its presence felt, but it was generally side by side with the nationalist struggle and was mixed with it, not alien to it. The Communist Party of India had been founded in 1925, but its identity was often the same as the Indian National Congress, the main political party in the country at that time. Nevertheless, life in Amritsar ran to a sweet, slow tenor, and the young Faiz could indulge in discussion and debate with his young friends, read voraciously and compose poetry. The tradition of the mushaira was strong and poetry was still something of a public affair at that time. Even Iqbal, whose poetry was philosophical and complex, was as much a public figure in the Amritsar of the 1930s as any major political leader like Mahatma Gandhi.

Poetry recitation at small or large gatherings inevitably led young poets to do 'more of the same'. Suggestions from and even participation by the audience in such recitations gave poetry a reality and a place in public life which now seems to have been appropriated by the film song.

The All India Radio, founded in 1930, was also becoming a medium to disseminate and share music and poetry among large audiences. Faiz must have felt inspired to compose more and more. In spite of the largely conventional image that Urdu poetry had at that time, patriotic fervour was bound to make its appearance in any poetry being written at that time. Urdu was no exception and, in fact, led the field in patriotic songs and poetry. In their twenties at that time, Faiz and his friends and peers felt the urge to come up with a line of thought capable of not just combating the colonial presence in the motherland but also of making a stand against the forces of communalism.

The struggle against poverty and the fight against the forces of capitalism gave young Faiz's poetry a sense of direction. The fight against political and social exploitation provided a common platform for poets who did not recognize the Hindu–Muslim divide, a divide which could have been a concern in Faiz's poetic imagination. But a common platform for the larger struggle for freedom and social change made communal consciousness irrelevant and superficial. The Marxist ideology, which gave primacy to economic and social forces governing human life in history, and which regarded the struggle for emancipation through revolution an imperative of history rather than a transcendental view of time and change, served the cause of communal harmony well, leading to the rejection of parochial concerns which seemed to be fanning the fires of communalism in those times.

By 1939, Faiz had made a name for himself in poetic circles. By that time he was also spending his time mingling with the working class, teaching them how to read and write and also refining their political sensibilities.

It is an interesting fact of Indian social history that the Muslim leftist intellectuals of those times came mostly from affluent families, or in fact even from what could be described as 'the ruling elite'. Brought up in the shadow of the Russian Revolution and nurtured on the populist notions of the French Revolution, they felt drawn to Marxism because of their dissatisfaction with the sociopolitical structure of the times, the oppressiveness of the British rule and a strong sense of the need for change. They were inveterate idealists, and though they were later derided for being 'armchair socialists' who wouldn't soil their hands with the sordid dirt of real life, they were true dreamers and idealists. Some well-known names among them are Sajjad Zaheer, Rashid Jahan, Mahmud-uz Zafar, Z.A. Ahmed, Muhammad Habeeb, Sibt-e Hasan, Kaifi Azmi, Sardar Jafri, Muhammad Ashraf, Abdul Aleem and Faiz himself. These wealthy or upper-middle-class intellectuals belonged to different regions but shared the same ideology and the same dream: the world needed to be changed, and Marxism was the force that could bring about the change. The Progressive Writers' Movement, founded in 1935 in London by Sajjad Zaheer and Mulk Raj Anand, among others, was the literary form of that dream.

To be sure, both Ideology and Dream suffered many shocks in the years to come. The first one was the ugly, nakedly imperialist truth of the pact between Stalin and Hitler which in any case couldn't prevent Hitler from invading the Soviet Union. But that truth was revealed later; the Soviet war and Hitler's comeuppance in that war came before. Yet, the Communist Party of India didn't pause to consider why Stalin didn't join the war against Hitler as other Western nations had done. The war was viewed in communist circles as an 'imperial war', which perhaps it was not, but which quickly became the 'War against Fascism' when Hitler invaded Soviet Russia in 1941.

The Nazi invasion of the Soviet Union gave the Progressives the opportunity to express their sense of shock and dismay and protest by joining the British Indian Army. By doing so, Faiz had joined the war against fascism, fighting the oppressors, siding with the oppressed. Then came Indian independence. His poem 'Subh-e Azaadi' (The dawn of freedom, August 1947) records the disappointment that he personally, and the communists as a party, felt with the way things ultimately turned out for the Indian subcontinent. The Partition served a massive blow, not just to leftist ideals but also to the Progressive Writers' Movement. When Gandhi was assassinated by a Hindu fanatic, Faiz expressed his sense of deep loss by actually attending Gandhi's funeral in Delhi, despite the fact that Hindu–Muslim relations at that time were more fraught with tension than ever before in history.

Freedom and Its Aftermath

The poem 'The Dawn of Freedom, August 1947' expresses disappointment and sorrow on two levels: the Partition and the carnage that accompanied it, and the disappointment that the freedom that came that morning was not a freedom brought by an armed revolution by the people and was therefore incomplete. True to his poetic voice, Faiz expressed his meaning through metaphors which are ambiguous in their nature anyway and seemed even more ambiguous in the context. It began thus:

> This light, smeared and spotted, this night-bitten dawn
> This isn't surely the dawn we waited for so eagerly

If the beginning was accusatory and melancholy, its end was some sort of a call to continue the struggle for the revolution:

> The weight of the night hasn't lifted yet
> The moment for the emancipation of the eyes
>   and the heart hasn't come yet
> Let's go on, we haven't reached the destination yet

Not unexpectedly, the poem drew a stinging rebuke from Sardar Jafri, the 'official' spokesman of Progressive literary thought at that time. He blamed Faiz for being 'too metaphorical', hence ambiguous, and praised Kaifi Azmi's poem on the same theme which, he once famously said, had 'a hortatory and rhetorical voice'.

In February 1947, Faiz became the editor of two dailies in Lahore: the *Pakistan Times* (in English) and the *Imroz* (in Urdu). Faiz was also active in the trade union movement and acted upon his beliefs to a very large extent. In 1951, he became the vice president of the Trade Union Congress, the labour wing of the Communist Party of Pakistan. The Pakistan government sent him to San Francisco in 1948 and to Geneva in 1949–50 as a part of the Pakistani government's delegation to the International Labour Organization.

Things seemed to be going well for Faiz for a while—until he was arrested in March 1951 in connection with the Rawalpindi Conspiracy case.[1] He was held in solitary confinement for three months in Sargodha and Lyallpur, where he was even deprived of writing material. It was during this period that he composed the following poem:

My pen and tablet, all that I had
Taken away from me
But what's there to grieve for?
For I have dipped my fingers in my heart's blood
So what if my lips have been sealed shut?
I have now put a tongue in
Each and every link of the chain

Denied pen and paper, Faiz had to commit this verse to memory even as he composed it. This poem exhibits a successful mingling of the classical flavour and revolutionary fervour with which Faiz infused his poetry. It was eventually published later in his collection *Dast-e Saba* (The touch of the breeze, *Nuskha Ha-e Wafa*, p. 107).

In 1953, Faiz was transferred to Hyderabad (Sindh) jail. He was released in April 1955 on bail and acquitted in September that year. Faiz's years in prison have been described in detail by Major Muhammad Ishaq, a fellow 'conspirator' and inmate in jail. The account serves well to construct the image of Faiz as the great revolutionary poet, struggling against odds but moving unflinchingly towards the realization of heroic dreams. During the period of his imprisonment, Faiz's poems had been ingeniously smuggled out of prison or else sent out with his letters and circulated widely. Hence, by the time of his release, Faiz had become a local celebrity, rather, a 'people's hero', with his verses being recited in almost every household across Pakistan.

Faiz was again imprisoned during the period of Ayyub Khan's martial law in 1958. However, it was not easy to keep him in jail this time as many in the military regime itself had become admirers of his poetry, and he was released after five months. He was awarded the Lenin Peace Prize in 1962. This prize, regarded as the equivalent of the Nobel Peace Prize, was widely acclaimed in the Indian subcontinent. According to Faiz himself, this was a humbling experience for him. I quote a major part of the latter part of his acceptance speech here:[2]

A few days ago when the world was resounding with the latest Soviet achievement in space, it occurred to me time and again that today when we can observe our world by taking a seat in the world of stars, then these petty meannesses, these selfish actions and these attempts to divide into parts and grasp the essentially small tracts of lands known as countries and the desire to make our writ run among small groups of people—how distant from rationality and reason these things are. Now that the paths of the universe are wide open before us and the treasures of the whole world can easily be under the control of human hands, is there still not present even a small number of people among us who are reasonable, just and honest, who can make everyone agree to wind up military installations, to sink in the ocean the bombs and rockets, the guns and cannons? And let us all, instead of trying to rule one another, go to conquer the universe where there is no shortage of space, where none needs to engage another in battle, where the environment is unlimited and where there are countless worlds. I am quite certain that in spite of all obstruction and difficulties, we will be able to make our human brotherhood agree to this suggestion.

I'm quite certain that humanity, which its enemies could never defeat, will yet be victorious, and instead of war and hatred, cruelty and malice, the foundation of a commonwealth will be shown to be the same which had been preached by Persian poet Hafiz long ago:

Whatever edifice you see in this world is prone to
defects and disturbance
It is only the edifice of love which is free of the taint
of defects and disturbance

Poetry and Revolution

Faiz published eight volumes of poetry in his lifetime. He wrote forewords to the first four. His poetry was well-received among scholars and readers abroad, and quite early on he began to be translated into English. At home, he quickly became (and remains) a major favourite of prominent ghazal singers of the subcontinent. He was written and talked about widely—and not only among the Progressives. The Englishman Victor Kiernan's extensive translation of his poems into English opened the door for the appreciation of Faiz in the international arena.[3] It is generally regarded as the premier work on Faiz Ahmed Faiz in English. Some other important translators of Faiz after Kiernan are by Shiv K. Kumar, Naomi Lazard and Agha Shahid Ali. Among those who extended the appreciation of Faiz abroad, mention must also be made of Ralph Russell, Frances Pritchett and Lyudmila Vasilyeva. The latter's work is available in both Russian and Urdu.

Naqsh-e Fariyaadi (The supplicant's portrait), Faiz's first collection of poems, was published in 1941. He published his second collection, *Dast-e Saba* (The touch of the breeze), in 1952. Both collections are slim; in fact, all his collections are small, and even then they contain some unfinished poems. This paucity of production may have added to the zeal and enthusiasm for his poetry. Every new poem was a cultural–literary event.

The second collection consists of poems written mostly when Faiz was active on the sociopolitical scene. The poems in *Zindaan Nama* (Prison chronicle), the third collection published in 1956, were mostly written during his imprisonment. It would be difficult to deny the influence of imprisonment on Faiz's mind and, by extension, on his poetry. In the preface to *Dast-e Saba*, Faiz discussed the impact of imprisonment on his development as a poet. Though the richness of his poetry undoubtedly transcends the mere fact of his imprisonment or the circumstances surrounding it, the confinement nevertheless has burnished Faiz's image as a heroic figure in the eyes of future generations of readers and listeners.

In 1956, when he was invited to attend the inaugural session of a conference of Asian writers organized in New Delhi by the Progressive Writers' Movement, Faiz was glowingly lauded as a champion of peace and universal brotherhood, a messiah of the working class. Among those present at the conference were Mulk Raj Anand, Sajjad Zaheer, Krishan Chandar and many other great names of the Progressive pantheon. In Sajjad Zaheer's words:

> If the evolution and progress of a culture were to be defined by the way the human race has rid itself of materialistic and spiritual destitution, and made its heart soft and malleable, its vision oriented towards truth and justice, and developing strength and elevation in its character, thus making our life pure and fragrant both internally and externally and also individually and collectively, then the poetry of Faiz can be said to have made a serious effort to achieve all of these cultural objectives.

There is no doubt that Faiz's poetry espouses the ideals of revolution, and that it talks of a life fraught with dangers. On a personal and also societal level, his poems evoke the threat of exploitation, both social and economic, the rule of a power-hungry tyranny, the elimination and destruction of the weak and innocent at the hands of the forces of tyranny/capitalism. Many poems in *Zindaan Nama* were written by him in response to political events taking place in the wider world. Hence, several international incidents or concerns—Iran, Israel, Africa, the arms' race between the nations—figure in his poems again and again.

The poem 'Hum Jo Taareek Raahon Mein Maare Gaye' (We who were put to death on dark roads, *Nuskha Ha-e Wafa*, p. 266) was written in 1954 after Faiz read the letters of Julius and Ethel Rosenberg, and is particularly moving. However, such is the poem's versatility and power that it can quite easily be severed from the cord that connects it with the immediate circumstances that triggered its writing:

Because we loved the flowers of your lips, we
Sacrificed ourselves on the dry stalk of the gibbet
Pining for the tapers of your hands, we
Were put to death on half-dark roads

Far from our lips hung on the gibbets
The ruby red of your lips kept leaping higher
The intoxication of your tresses kept falling like the rain
The silver of your hands gleamed and glistened

When your paths became saturated with the tyrannies'
    evening

We began to march; we marched as far as our steps
    could take us
The words of a ghazal on our lips, the candle of pain
    burning in our hearts

This is also manifest in one of his ghazals published in
Zindaan Nama (Prison chronicle, *Nuskha Ha-e Wafa,*
p. 248), which begins: 'Some is supplied to the secret
assemblies of the censors . . .'

Faiz says:

Yes, I know, I too fear for my life
But what can one do?
Every road that leads to where I want to go
passes through the execution ground

However, while Faiz is widely hailed as a poet of the revolution,
it needs to be stressed that his love poems are as good as or
even better than his poems of protest against tyranny. In fact,
many of his poems which can neither be classified as love
poems nor poems of political activism are as good as any in
all of modern Urdu poetry. Notwithstanding the shibboleth
that it is criminal according to the Progressives to ever be in
despair, some of Faiz's poems do lack in hope and yet they

make beautiful, if despairing, depictions of reality. One such poem ranked very high by literary critics is 'Tanhaai' (Solitude, *Nuskha Ha-e Wafa*, p. 71):

Did somebody come again, sad heart?
No, nobody
It must be a wayfarer somewhere, he'll go away
The night is past, the stardust begins to dissipate
The still lamps in the mansions begin to falter
Weary of waiting, all the roads are now in slumber
The dusty road, unsympathetic, has clouded all traces of
    footprints
Put out the lamps; remove the wine, the jug and the goblet!
Lock your sleepless doors
No one, no one's going to come here now

Faiz's experiments with poetic forms also extend to the ghazal. It has often been said that in the field of the ghazal, Faiz's greatest achievement was to revive the classical ghazal's frequently used words and phrases which had lost much of their charm or meaning by the time Faiz and other modern writers came on the scene. It must, however, be borne in mind that the bulk of the imagery and vocabulary that has given meaningful resonance to the classical ghazal is part of a whole system of meanings and associations. These associations—or what may be termed as the 'hinterland of meaning'—are what gives force and resonance to apparently trite words like *shama* (candle), *parwaana* (moth), *dar* (scaffold), *maqtal* (execution ground) and so forth. It was recognized by Samuel Taylor Coleridge long before the advent of the modernists that the meaning of a word consists not only of its dictionary definitions but also the associations that it conjures up before us. Thus, the achievement of Faiz does not consist in his giving new life to a dead body of images; actually, it consists in the power and appeal of the message that he desired to convey. The message was to make the audience or reader understand and appreciate both the hazard and the romance of revolution. He wanted, and he succeeded in great measure, to present the idea of revolution enveloped in the attractive mist of sacrifice leading to social change, if not the emancipation of the oppressed of the world.

In fact, Faiz resisted the temptation of his admirers to dub him as a poet with a revolutionary message. Quite unlike Iqbal, he desired to be known as a poet, not a torchbearer. In the preface to his collection *Dast-e Tah-e Sang* (A hand trapped under a block of stone), he says:

I don't really like talking about myself. For example, I don't use the first person singular in my poetry as far as possible. Instead of the pronoun 'I', I always prefer to use the pronoun 'We'. Thus, when literary investigators and detectives sit down to ask me: 'Why do you write poetry? How do you write poetry? What is the purpose for which you write poetry?', then in order just to let the matter slide, I reply with whatever comes to my mind. For example I say, 'Well, you should yourself look for these things in my poetry and seek the answers to how I write and for what purpose I write.'

The Classical and the Modern

The early modern poet and freedom fighter Hasrat Mohani (1875–1951), whom Faiz greatly admired, wrote thus about the nature of poetry:

> True poems, O Hasrat, are only those
> Which should affect the heart the moment they are heard

Hasrat's verse recalls a point often made in the pre-modern (or 'classical') literary discourse. As we know, the poetics of the classical or the pre-modern ghazal recognizes a quality of poetry which was described as *kaifiyat* (loosely, mood). Kaifiyat implies that quality of the poem which causes the reader or the hearer to pay greater attention to that emotional affect which immediately arises in the mind or the heart and which has no direct connection to the actual meaning of the poem. Perhaps it is something similar to what T.S. Eliot described when he said that poetry may often communicate itself before it is understood. But it should be obvious that the creation of kaifiyat could not come to pass without giving due stress to the fundamental technical requirements of the verse. For example, the two lines of the verse should be fully connected and there should be a bedrock of meaning; there should be no wasteful use of words, and it would be even more desirable if the words have affinities with each other. Thus the condition of kaifiyat was not satisfied by just creating an emotional affect.

Early modern critics like Hasrat Mohani and Masud Hasan Rizvi Adeeb, who professed to belong to this tradition, have, however, not made any mention of kaifiyat (which, as we can see, is a complicated concept). The reason for their silence on the matter of kaifiyat perhaps was that in the eyes of these critics—as is evident from the words of Hasrat Mohani quoted above—the purpose of poetry was to cause an immediate emotional response. The content of the poem should be to move the heart; that was enough. They tried to express this idea in many ways, invoking phrases like 'authenticity of emotion' or 'recreating the poet's own feelings in the heart of the reader'; they also advocated that 'autobiographical' or 'interior' events ought to be described in such a way that 'they should seem universal', and so forth.

The poetry of Faiz draws much of its power from its imagery. It is also full of kaifiyat-like atmosphere, though it's not true according to the Progressives. By way of example, here are the opening lines of his celebrated poem 'A Morning in the Prison House' from *Dast-e Saba* (The touch of the breeze, *Nuskha Ha-e Wafa*, p. 181)

A bit of the night still remained when the moon
    came to my bedside
And said, 'Awake, morning is here
Awake, for the wine of sleep that was your share is shrunk
to the bottom of the wine cup.'
Bidding farewell to the beloved's image, I opened my eyes
And looked at the sheet of the night's dark, still water

The imagery of Faiz, which has its share of metaphor, adds to the power and effect of these lines. The following three lines, which have an almost magical effect, follow the first four lines of the poem under discussion:

Whirlpools of silver began to dance everywhere
And star lamps falling from the hands of the moon
Drowning, floating, wilting and blooming
Night and morning clung in a long embrace

These lines have no role to play in establishing the character of the poem. Even a brief reflection will show that these lines are in fact devoid of meaning but succeed as lines of verse because of the power and brilliance of the imagery. The beauty of the imagery, its immediate effect, its novelty, these are the jewels that adorn the crown of Faiz's perfection. This is something like kaifiyat here, but not quite kaifiyat because the bedrock of meaning and the coherence between the lines are not quite there. Still, the poem succeeds because of its emotional affect, not because of what it says in actual words.

Very few people have understood the fact that the flowing, limpid musicality of Faiz's poetry has played an important role in extending his reach among ordinary as well as sophisticated readers. Khusrau has very subtle and delectable discussions on this limpid musicality or 'flowingness' in his prefaces. In Arabic too, much before Persian, *rawaani*, or the ability to flow smoothly, has been described as an important felicity in poetry. That no definition had ever been attempted of rawaani is perhaps beside the point. The reason could be that rawaani or flowingness can only be felt—it cannot be described or defined. Like the metricality of the poem, this ability to flow smoothly is also something that defies proof of its existence. Just as metricality is universally recognized and accepted as a basic quality of poetry (Coleridge has even gone to the extent of saying that the very nature of poetry is such that it demands metricality), so also the rawaani of a poem is a universally acknowledged fact. The Arab philosopher Al Farabi made the point in a different way when he said that the musicality of a metrical utterance is its natural attribute.

In Arab literary culture, composing poems and then reciting them aloud were both held in equal importance. One was also taught how to recite *sher*s (or poetry) there. Khalil Ibn Ahmad has described a poem to be essentially a collection of sounds. A little later, the Arab poet and theorist Jahiz makes a discussion on rawaani which he concludes by saying that an utterance could be regarded as rawaani when an entire line sounds like a word and a word sounds like just one tone. The poetry of Faiz is perhaps the best flowing among all the modern poets.

Another thing that strikes me as important about Faiz is that he makes us participate in the act of his poem but does not burden us with any responsibility to act. Far less trying to persuade us to action or struggle or march on the path of revolution, he doesn't even give a message to us. His revolution, or the struggle for the revolution, includes us as partner but makes no demands on us. Faiz does not ever force or compel or persuade us; he never preaches to us. The protagonist in his poems, both nazms and ghazals, may occasionally strike us as sad or melancholy but he's mainly a witness or messenger. He places no burden on us that we too side with the protagonist or with the forces engaged in the struggle for the revolution. Thus, we become participants in the revolution or the struggle for it without actually taking part in it.

Friedrich Nietzsche put forth a very important point when he said that if you gaze for too long into the abyss, the abyss will start to gaze back at you. What he really meant was that the act of seeing or hearing is not one-sided. Faiz's poetry does not preach or try to persuade us to act. Rather, it makes us take part in the act anyway. Look at these closing lines of 'Ay Raushniyon Ke Shahr' (O city of lights!, *Nuskha Ha-e Wafa*, p. 262) from *Zindaan Nama*:

> May the beloveds, the Lailahs that dwell there be
> ever safe!
> Let someone go tell them:
> Tonight, when you light up the lamps,
> Turn the wicks up as far as they can go

The last line flows so smoothly and is so dramatic that our critical sense is blunted when we confront its magic. But when we read closely we realize that the word 'Lailahs', though extremely beautiful and heart-affecting—conjuring as it does the image of beautiful young women active in support of the revolution—has no real content. It is never made clear that there are indeed Lailahs in the city. Perhaps there are nothing but witches there because the City of Lights is hidden behind the dark surrounding wall of disunion. Even so, we accept that there are Lailahs there. Their faces are bright and their garments are bright and they light lamps in the city, perhaps on its surrounding walls. In the poem, somebody is being asked to tell the Lailahs that they should keep the lamps burning brightly. It is clear that we have no role to play here. The messenger to the Lailahs is someone unknown and we have no responsibility for him. Is it that the hands of the Lailahs are now paralysed? We don't know. Nor does the protagonist know anything about it. Is there any danger to the girls who are being asked to burn the lamps brightly? We don't know and neither does the protagonist of the poem.

All this is very well. Yet, we still share the anxiety of the protagonist that 'the flood of desire' (a rather filmi expression, to be sure) may not be repulsed by the invasion of the attackers by night. We are sincerely and ardently sure that there are Lailahs behind the dark surrounding wall and it is their job and function to keep the lamps burning brightly. We have to do nothing. The protagonist also has to do nothing but to state what is to be done. Even then, having read the poem or having heard it recited before us, we too become fighters in the battle against the attackers by night.

Conclusion

I have no qualms in saying that had Faiz not been so diligently mindful of the poetics of the Progressive movement, his poetic universe would have been even more diverse and colourful. But I would also say that by giving primacy to metaphor and imagery, Faiz was able to give the kind of power to his poetry which has otherwise been out of bounds for much Progressive poetry in Urdu. The reason for this could also be that he had an acute sense of compassion for the individual, the solitary and lonely being whose fears and anxieties we all share but who remains unknown to the world. Faiz is not a poet of the teeming crowd, the so-called 'people'. Rather, he's a poet who speaks for the lonely, the single human being. Had this not been so, the sense of the individual's centrality and the truth of individual experiences would not have been so evident in his poetry. We become more aware of our own relevance and importance when we read Faiz.

There's no poet in Urdu poetry other than Mir Taqi Mir who has a deeper awareness of the individual as the self, the 'I' who can't always be a part of the world of 'Not I'. There's this person who listens to no one but himself and of course does his own thing. He's at no one's beck and call, not even the beloved's. Just hear, this Mir:

It's very hard for you to find someone like me
Yet of course, dear beloved, it's so easy to kill me
I am the one, do you hear? Who would stop somewhere
    and die
Is it that you believe it to my vocation always to wander
    from street to street?
The total world-ness of the two worlds sinks and
    floats here—
My heart, just a clot of blood, is a flood in itself

Faiz's sense of deprivation and complaint does not allow him to reach these heights, but he also doesn't let slip any opportunity to acknowledge his own importance as an individual. Faiz gives us the strength to not regard ourselves as just 'a repeated letter on the world's slate' (in Ghalib's phrase) that can be erased by anyone at the whim of his will.

The poem that Faiz wrote in memory of Iqbal (Iqbal, *Nuskha Ha-e Wafa,* p. 85) rings true for Faiz himself:

To our land came a sweet-singing fakir
And lost in thought, he went away singing his melodies
The untrodden paths came alive with people

The dormant fortunes of desolate wine-houses came awake
There were just a few eyes that actually caught sight of him
But his song permeated every heart

Today, when the Word is in danger at the hands of the demagogue, the traducer of the reality of loneliness and pain, when the dignity of the individual is at stake and the freedom of speech much at risk of fast becoming an obsolete concept, we need the poetry of Faiz more than ever before. One is reminded of Eliot:

The Word within the word
Unable to speak a word

Faiz stood for the dignity of man, the holiness of pain, the constructive power of the word and the sanctity of individual belief. He will always be needed, and that is his triumph and our tragedy.

Notes

1. The Rawalpindi Conspiracy case was an attempt to overthrow the government of Pakistan in 1951. All the

conspirators were arrested in March 1951 and sentenced to long terms of imprisonment. The conspiracy was led by Major General Akbar Khan, and included Major General Nazir Ahmad and many others from the army and the air force. Three left-oriented or communist civilians were also involved in the conspiracy. They were: Faiz Ahmed Faiz, poet; Sajjad Zaheer, critic and ideologue of the Progressive Movement; and Muhammad Husain Ata. They were defended by the famous lawyer-politician Huseyn Shaheed Suhrawardy, who, after becoming prime minister of Pakistan in 1956, obtained reprieve for most of the conspirators. Faiz and Sajjad Zaheer were released much earlier. Sajjad Zaheer returned to India while Faiz remained in Pakistan and continued his career as a left-wing poet and intellectual.

2. Quotations have been taken from the introductions provided in *Nuskha Ha-e Wafa* and translated into English by the translator herself. See: Faiz Ahmed Faiz, *Nuskha Ha-e Wafa: Kulliyat-e Faiz* (Delhi: Farid Book Depot, 1997).

3. Victor Kiernan, *Poems by Faiz* (London: George Allen & Unwin, 1971).

POEMS SELECTED FROM

Naqsh-e Fariyaadi

1

View (1)

Doors, windows and rooftops, crushed under the
    weight of silence
A stream of pain flowing from the sky
The story of the moon's light filled with sorrow and grief
Roiled in the dust of the highways
A dim darkness in bedrooms
The feeble tune of the sitar of existence
Singing elegies in soft tones

2

Beloved, Don't Ask Me for the Love That Was

Don't ask me to love you the way I did before, my love
I'd imagined life to be bright and glowing because
    you were in it
What cared I for sorrows other than the joys of pining
    in your love?
It's your beauty that keeps springtime intact upon the world
What else remains to be sought in the universe but your eyes?
I would conquer fate, were you to be mine
I had thought of it like this, if only like a passing fancy

There are other sorrows in this world than love
There are other pleasures than lovers' meeting

The dark oppressive shadows of countless centuries
Woven into the narratives of the wealthy
Bodies being traded, clandestinely or brazenly
Roiled in the dust, soaked in blood

My glance cannot help falling on those things too
Your beauty remains an attractive proposition, but, no!

There are sorrows other than love in this world to care for
Other pleasures than the joy of union with the beloved
Don't ask me to love you the way I did before, my love

3

Ghazal

Having Lost the Two Worlds to Your Love

Having lost the two worlds to your love
There goes someone after his night of sorrow

The wine-house deserted, the wine casks and glasses sad
The spring sulks and refuses to come
ever since you went away

We were given a chance to err but just for a few days
I know the kind of nerve the mighty Creator has!

The world made me a stranger to your memory

The sorrows of time turned out to be more
    alluring than you

O Faiz! She smiled at me today quite by accident
Now don't ask about the schemes spun by my
    inexperienced heart

4

Solitude

Did somebody come again, sad heart?
No, nobody
It must be a wayfarer somewhere, he'll go away
The night is past, the stardust begins to dissipate
The still lamps in the mansions begin to falter
Weary of waiting, all the roads are now in slumber
The dusty road, unsympathetic, has clouded all
     traces of footprints
Put out the lamps; remove the wine, the jug and the goblet!
Lock your sleepless doors
No one, no one's going to come here now

5

A Few Days More, My Love

A few days more, my love, just a few days
Breathing the air under the shadow of tyranny
Suffering cruelty, injustice, weeping some more
We are doomed, crippled by our inheritance
With caged bodies and chained emotions
Imprisoned are our thoughts, and utterances censored
Just staying alive speaks of our courage
Is life nothing but the tattered gown of a
    poverty-stricken man
On which is added every moment a new patch of pain?
But tyranny's term is now due to depart
A little more forbearance, and our days of
    complaint are numbered

In this scorched wilderness of time's desert
We have to live, but no longer the same
We may have to put up with the heavy, nameless
    tyranny of alien hands
Today, but not forever
Misfortune's dust clings to your radiant body
Witnesses to youth that lasted but a day or two
The futile smouldering pain of moonlit nights
The ineffectual throb of the heart, the call of the
    despairing body
A few days more, my love, just a few days

6

The Death of the Fires of Love

Come, let's celebrate the passing of the passion of love
Come, let's burn our hearts with the cold beauty
    of the moon
Let's rejoice in the pangs of separation from the
    beloved's frame and figure
Let's punish our sight with the sight of the cypress
    and the rose and the jasmine
Make the desolate life even more desolate
Let me heed your advice for once, dear counsellor
Sheltered again under the hem of spring's rain
Soothe and placate the heart at times, shed tears at times
Untie listlessly the tangled knots of such questions:
Should I go there, or not go; not go at all or go for real?

Preach to the heart yet again the doctrine of restraint
And again avoid testing the resolve to be patient
Come, for the story of passion has concluded today
Let us now narrate the tales of love's ceasing to be

7

Speak

Speak, for your lips are free
Speak, for your tongue is still yours
Your upright body belongs to you
Speak, for your soul still is yours
Look, how in the blacksmith's shop
The embers are hot, the iron glows
The mouths of the locks are being opened
Chains lengthen their reach
Speak, for the little time that you have is sufficient
Before the death of body and tongue
Speak, for the truth still lives
Speak, say all that is to be said

8

Iqbal

To our land came a sweet-singing fakir
And, lost in thought, he went away singing his melodies
The untrodden paths came alive with people
The dormant fortunes of desolate wine-houses came awake
There were just a few eyes that actually caught sight of him
But his song permeated every heart

The kingly fakir is now gone far into the distance
Once again are the paths of our land plunged into gloom
His special elegance of mind remembered by a handful
A couple of his glances and gestures
Live in the minds of a few loved ones
But his song resides in every heart

And there are numerous who still relish
the flavour of its tune

All the beauties of the song are immortal
Its plenitude, its energy, its passion
The song is hot and piercing, like a whirling blaze
Its flame can sear the heart of the wind of death
Like a lamp oblivious of the wild, boisterous wind
Or like a light of the night's assembly
uncaring about the morning's approach

9

Highway

A long, desolate highway
Its gaze fixed on the far horizon
Spreading out its grey beauty
On the breast of the cold earth—
Like a grief-stricken woman
In her desolate home
Dreaming of her absent lover
Lost in thought, each part of her body immersed
in the idea of union

POEMS SELECTED FROM

Dast-e Saba

10

Poem

My pen and tablet, all that I had
Taken away from me
But what's there to grieve for?
For I have dipped my fingers in my heart's blood
So what if my lips have been sealed shut?
I have now put a tongue in
each and every link of the chain

11

My Companion, My Friend

If I was sure, my companion, my friend
If I was sure the weariness in your heart
The sadness in your eyes and the burning in your breast
Can be dispelled by my comforting words, my love
Were my words of solace a medic which
could bring back to life your desolate and extinguished mind
Washing away the stain of humiliation from your forehead
and cure your ailing youth
If I was sure, my companion, my friend

Day through night, morning through evening
I would spend whiling away your pain
Singing to you light, melodious songs

Of spring, gardens and waterfalls
Of sunrise, of the moon and the planets
I would tell you tales of beauty and love
I'd tell you how
Unresponsive bodies of proud, snow-moulded women
Melt under the heat of passionate hands
How the stable contours of a familiar face
Change shape in an instant
How the crystal-bright visage of a beloved
Flushes red with a sip of the ruby red wine
How the rose branch offers itself to the flower-picker
How the night's mansion becomes fragrant
I would sing to you, go on singing for you
Weaving songs for you, always around you
But my songs are not the cure for your grief
Melodies may not be surgeons, though they
can be friends and sympathizers
Songs may not be lancets, though
They can be a salve for pain at least
There's no help for your affliction but the knife
And that cruel blood-letter is not in my power
Not in any earthly being's power
Except you yourself, you, only you

12

The Dawn of Freedom, August 1947

This light, smeared and spotted, this night-bitten dawn
This isn't surely the dawn we waited for so eagerly
This isn't surely the dawn with whose desire cradled
    in our hearts
We had set out, friends all, hoping
We should somewhere find the final destination
Of the stars in the forests of heaven
The slow-rolling night must have a shore somewhere
The boat of the afflicted heart's grieving will drop
    anchor somewhere

When from the mysterious paths of youth's hot blood
The young fellows moved out

Numerous were the hands that rose to clutch
the hems of their garments
Open arms called, bodies entreated
from the impatient bedchambers of beauty—

But the yearning for the dawn's face was too dear
The hem of the radiant beauty's garment was very close
The load of desire wasn't too heavy
Exhaustion lay somewhere on the margin

It's said the darkness has been cleft from light already
It's said the journeying feet have found union
    with the destination
The protocols of those who held the pain in their
    hearts have changed now
Joy of union—yes; agony of separation—forbidden!

The burning of the liver, the eyes' eagerness, the heart's grief
Remain unaffected by this cure for disunion's pain
From where did the beloved, the morning breeze come?
    Where did it go?
The street lamp at the edge of the road has no notion yet

The weight of the night hasn't lifted yet
The moment for the emancipation of the eyes
    and the heart hasn't come yet
Let's go on, we haven't reached the destination yet

13

Ghazal
The Tablet and the Pen

I will go on nurturing the tablet and the pen
I'll go on recording what the heart goes through

I'll go on providing wherewithal to love's passion
I'll keep being kind to the desolation of the times

No doubt, the harshness of the times will grow even worse
No doubt, the tyrants will continue to practise tyranny

I accept the harshness, I bear this torture
I'll go on trying to remedy the affliction with every breath

Long live the wine-house, with the wine's fiery red colour
I'll go on decorating the doors and balconies of holy spaces

So long as there's blood in my heart, with my tears
I'll go on creating the colours of the beloved's face

Her way is unmindfulness, so she's free to cultivate it
And I have to voice my longing, so I'll go on doing it

14

Ghazal
As Soon As the Wounds of
Your Memory Begin to Heal

As soon as the wounds of your memory begin to heal
I begin to remember you on some excuse or the other

When the manners of talking about the beloved
    begin to brighten
Tresses in every beloved's chamber begin to be coiffed
    and made up

Every stranger seems familiar to me
When I pass through your street, even now

Strangers away from home, when they speak of their country
To the morning breeze, the dawn's eyes well up with tears

Whenever they control our speech by stapling our lips
The atmosphere resounds even more with songs of freedom

As darkness seals the doors of the prison house, O Faiz
Stars rise to illuminate the heart

15

To Your Beauty

The poet composes salutations to your beauty
When the colours of someone's garment are sprinkled
    on the terrace
The morning is brightened sometimes, or the afternoon,
    or the evening
And if a dress beautifies itself on someone's elegant stature
The cypress and the pine in the garden have found
    fresh grace
The ghazal began to take shape when the heart dipped
    the wine glass
in the reflection of your lips and face

The poet composes salutations to your beauty—

So long as the henna's colour on your palms retains
its brightness
There remains in the world the art of how to love the bride
called poetry
So long as your beauty has its youthful power, the world is
kind to me
So long as you draw breath, the air of our land is our friend
Even if times are tough and misfortunes extreme
Your memory sweetens the bitterness of the times
The poet composes salutations to your beauty!

16

Ghazal
Colour, the Name of Your Dress

Colour: the name of your dress
perfume: the name of your hair flowing in the wind
The season of the flowers is the name of
your appearance on the balcony

Friends, say something about those eyes and lips
Without which the subject of the garden
nor the name of the wine-house can gain colour

The scent of flowers again fills my sight
and lamps begin to shine in the heart
Once again the imagination brings up the notion
of visiting her assembly

17

Ghazal

Your Forgotten Sorrows Wander Back into the Heart

Your forgotten sorrows wander back into the heart
Like the long-exiled idols tiptoeing into the Ka'aba

The stars brighten up one by one
Are those your feet moving towards this, my home?

Speed up the wine's dance! Enhance the music's pitch!
Look, ambassadors from the Ka'aba are on their way
    to the wine-house!

It's I who doesn't have the patience to bear
    her favour's gratuity

Actually, she's always inclined to kindness
    whenever she visits

Hey, let someone plead with disunion's night
    not to pass too fast
My heart aches not much right now, nor is her
    memory so importunate

18

The Heart's Wine Glass,
Once Broken, Can't Be Repaired

Pearl, bottle of wine, wine glass or pearl in an earring
Once broken, it stays broken
When have tears been able to join it together?
What's broken is gone, forever

Needlessly you pick up the shards
And gather them in the hem of your dress
There's none to bring the broken glass back to wholeness
On whom do you pin your hopes?

It's among those broken pieces perhaps
That there is the wine glass of the heart in which

The fairy of love's sorrow would pour itself
With a hundred cruel, coquettish airs

And then one day the world seized that wine glass
from you and smashed it into pieces
Spilt the wine into the dust and
Broke the kingly wings of the guest

These colourful particles belong perhaps
To those beautiful, crystalline dreams
Which embellished and enhanced
your private being in the drunken prime of youth

Deprivation, drudgery at work, hunger and grief
Dashed against those dreams
The four-pronged attack was merciless
What could the fragile structures of glass do?

Or perhaps among those slivers of glass somewhere
Is hidden the pearl of your honour
That which made even the tallest of them
Envy you when you were at your humblest

The treasure which was madly sought after
By many and merchant and robber
This is Thief City; here the destitute
Lose their name to save their life

Pearl, bottle of wine, wine glass or pearl in an earring
Fetch good prices only when whole
If in little slivers as they now are
They just stab and make you shed tears of blood

Needlessly you pick up the shards
And gather them in the hem of your dress
There's none to bring the broken glass back to wholeness
On whom do you pin your hopes?

You may darn the collar of memories
But that won't sustain the heart
Undoing a seam, sewing another
Is that the way a life can be lived?

In the workshop of life where
The wine glass and the bottle are cast
You can find a substitute for every thing
And can fill your every need

The hands that are stretched are successful
The eye that looked up, fortunate
There's no end to the riches here
However many highwaymen may lie in ambush

Can the marauding, plundering life ever
Empty the stores and warehouses?
There are mountains upon mountains of diamonds here
And oceans upon oceans of pearls

There are some who hide this wealth
Behind walls and curtains
Putting on the auctioneer's block
Every ocean, every mountain

But there are some who fight
And rip off the curtains
And place obstacles in the path of
Life's cut-purses

The two parties fight fierce battles, forever
In every neighbourhood, every town
In the heart of every home
On the forehead of every busy road

One smears blackness everywhere
The other lights lamps
One sets fire to things
The other quenches the fire

All wine glasses, bottles, rubies and pearls
are placed as bets in this game
Arise! For all the empty hands
are summoned to battle!

19

Ghazal

Let There Be Some Clouds,
Let There Be Some Wine

Let there be some clouds, let there be some wine
After this let there be whatever punishment there may be

Let the moon come down from the decanter's balcony
And the sun shine in the hand of the cup-bearer

Let every vein in the body light up like fire
Let the beloved appear unveiled once again

On every page of life the heart saw inscribed
Chapters of your love and fidelity

I was taking count of life's sorrows today
Your memories flooded my mind uncountably

The sovereignty of love's sorrows never went away
Though the heart witnessed revolutions every day!

The pillars and arches of the rival's assembly
burst into flame
Whenever the homeless like us happened to arrive there

My silence echoed everywhere so
As if every direction were in response

Every road, every path was the destination, Faiz
We arrived successful wherever we reached

20

An Evening in the Prison House

The night descending step by step
From the zigzag patterns
Of the evening stars
The gentle breeze passes softly
As if someone uttering words of love
The homeless trees of the courtyard of the prisonhouse
Bending, are absorbed in making floral patterns
On the skyscape
On the balcony's shoulder gleams
The beauteous hand of the gentle moonlight
The luminance of the stars has dissolved into the earth
And the indigo of the sky has dissolved into fluorescence
Bluish shadows flow in green corners

Like the surge of the wave of pain
Of disunion flowing into the heart

The mind tells the heart, again and again
How beautiful is life at this moment!
Those who decoct the poison of tyranny
Can never flourish, today nor tomorrow
So what if they have already
Extinguished the lights in the hall
Of union with the beloved?
I dare them to put out the moon!

21

A Morning in the Prison House

A bit of the night still remained when the moon
    came to my bedside
And said, 'Awake, morning is here.
Awake, for the wine of sleep that was your share
    is shrunk
to the bottom of the wine cup.'
Bidding farewell to the beloved's image, I opened my eyes
And looked at the sheet of the night's dark, still water

Whirlpools of silver began to dance everywhere
And star lamps falling from the hands of the moon
Drowning, floating, wilting and blooming
Night and morning clung in a long embrace

In the prison's courtyard
the golden aspects of friends and comrades
Emerged glistening from the dark surface, slowly
The dew of slumber had washed away
From their faces signs of sorrow for the homeland
And grief of distance from beauty's face

A gong sounded in the distance
Bored legs began doing their rounds
The prison guards, pale, afflicted by hunger
Angry, loud laments of the prison inmates
Roam around, arm in arm with the guards

The winds laden with the pleasure of sleep awakened
The poison-saturated cries of the prison house awakened
Far away somewhere a door opened, another
slammed shut
Far away somewhere a chain rattled, importunate, and wept
Far away somewhere a dagger thrust deep into
    a padlock's heart
A window began to strike its head violently over
    and over again
As if life's enemies were awoken from sleep

Ponderous djinns cast in iron and stone
In whose clutches complain night and day
The tender fairies of my useless days and nights
Imprisoned, they await the arrival of their royal firstborn
Whose quiver is full of arrows of incandescent hope

(Unfinished)

22

Remembrance

O life of the world! In the desert of loneliness throb
The shadows of your voice, the mirage of your lips
In the desert of loneliness
Buried under the dust and brambles of separation
flower the lilies and roses of your side

From somewhere close by
the warmth of your breath rises in the air
Smouldering in its own fragrance, softly, slowly
Far away, shining brightly on the horizon
Falls drop by drop the dew of your heart-warming glance

How lovingly, at this moment, O life of the world
Has your memory placed its hand on the face of my heart!
It seems to me, though it's a morning of disunion
The day of separateness is over
and the night of union has come

POEMS SELECTED FROM

Zindaan Nama

23

Meeting

(1)
This night is the tree of a pain
That is greater than you or me
Greater than us, for in its branches
Rows upon rows of torch-bearing stars
Have been surrounded and lost their light
A thousand moons, in its shade
Have wept away their moonlight
This night is the tree of a pain
That is greater than you or me
Yet it's from the tree of this night
that the yellow leaves of these few moments
Have fallen, and caught in your tresses
They have burst into colour

It's from the dew of this very night
that these few drops of silence
have fallen on your forehead
And have become a wreath of diamonds

(2)
This night is very dark, but
In this darkness shines out
That stream of blood which is my voice
It is in this shade that shines bright
The golden flow which is your gaze

The grief that smoulders at the present time
In the garden of your arms
(This grief which is the fruit of this night)
Were it to burn some more in the flame
of our burning sighs
would actually become a glowing ember

Each and every arrow that has been shot into the liver
From the bow of every black branch
We plucked out, we made each one
Into an axe

(3)
It is not in the heavens that the morning
Of the anguished and the grief-stricken will dawn
The bright face of morning will be seen
Right here, where we stand
It's here that the sparks blossomed from pain
Have bloomed crimson into a dawn
It's here that the weapons of murderous sorrows
Have turned into rows upon rows
Of garlands of fiery sunshine

The sorrow that was imparted by this night
The same sorrow has been the conviction for the morning
Conviction, which is of compassion more than sorrow
Morning, which is of greatness more than night

24

Ghazal

When Does the Memory of You Leave My Side?

When does the memory of you leave my side?
when do I not have your hand in mine?
A hundred thanks that in our nights
are not included any more the nights of separation

If things are difficult there can't we even sell off our hearts
give up our lives?
O keepers of hearts! Have things come to such a pass
in the beloved's quarters?

The attitude that you bear to the slaughter
is remembered after you
Who cares for this life?
After all, it is only a coming and going

The field of faithfulness is not someone's royal court
where your pedigree is questioned
Lover is not a name given to a person
nor is love a caste

If the wager is to be set for love
stake what you will fearlessly
If you were to win, how wonderful
losing is not so bad either

25

O City of Lights!

The insipid, pale noon sun dries up
sward by sward
The venom of loneliness is licking away at the walls
As far as the farthest horizon it keeps advancing
diminishing, rising, falling, like a fog
The turgid wave of colourless, uninteresting
    exertions and pains
And behind that fog there's the city of lights

O city of lights!
Who can tell which way lies the road to your lights?
For on all sides stands the dark city wall
    of disunion

Everywhere, the exhausted forces of love lie recumbent
My heart is troubled today
O city of lights!
I fear the flood of desire might be repulsed in a
        surprise attack by night—
May the beloveds, the Lailahs that dwell there be ever safe!
Let someone go tell them:
Tonight, when you light up the lamps
Turn the wicks up as far as they can go

26

Ghazal

Some Is Supplied to the Secret Assemblies

Some is supplied to the secret assemblies of the censors
and some is delivered to the preacher's house
Very little of what should be ours—the rightful share
    of the true drinkers—
falls into our wine cups

Did you ever see stone-hearts turn to water
by submitting words of desire, O heart of mine?
However much one may cultivate submission
did a tyrant ever change his ways?

It's the land of the unjust, no remedy here, no plaint possible
The suppliant's cry, if it's fool enough to rise
Breaks its head at the door
from door to door

Yes, I know, I too fear for my life
But what can one do?
Every road that leads to where I want to go
passes through the execution ground

Now the wayfarer to the beloved's street should be
highwayman too if he wishes to get there
Enemy-rivals don't budge from their station of the watch
and the night, it keeps passing steadily

Confined to the cage, we aren't all that alone, really
The morning breeze of home, every day
Arrives scented with memories and departs
    bright with tears

27

A Lover to a Beloved

This memory lane which you've been treading
in this manner for a long time now
Will come to an end should you go a few more steps
There's a bend there, that of the wilderness of forgetting
Beyond it, there's neither someone called I
Nor someone called you
Eyes watch with baited breath for who knows when
You'd return, or pass, or turn your head to look

Although the eyes are aware, all this is nought but illusion
Yet if ever somewhere the eyes held you in embrace
Another road would immediately foliate there

On which there'll again be, constantly in front of us
The journey of the caressing arm, the tresses' shade

That other thing is also false: the heart knows
There are no more bends, no wildernesses, no ambush
That I may be deceived into sinking my moon as they roll by
Better let this path be peopled by your tread as before
No matter
if you didn't even turn to look

POEMS SELECTED FROM

Dast-e Tah-e Sang

28

Hand Trapped under a Block of Stone

The surrounding air is out of humour, the morning breeze
    hell bent on causing hurt—
The fact of the matter:
each and every old comrade is annoyed

Hey, dear fellow drinkers, now the season is in full colour!
Now the manner of the environment is worth
    a trip outside!

From all sides, accusations shower down like the
    season of rains
Contumely's cloud swells in every direction

There's something poured in it
The flask of wine seems to smoulder
Every glass of wine is more than deadly poison

Hey, raise the glass, for in remembrance of honey lips
Friends have drunk this poison time and time again!

There's no retribution, nor reward
for the passion of the heart—
The objective of travelling down the path of love
is not requital of love nor the beloved's tyranny

To know the pain of the heart: that's the recompense
for the sorrow of love
And *that* is the consciousness of beauty
it's your bounty to us

Every morning that dawns over the garden
    is your spring-like face
Every flower is a footprint
    of your memory

Every drenched, descending night is
the dewdrop which is your braid of hair
The westering sun is the air around your lips

Every road ends at the door of your love
Every word of desire is the sound of your footsteps

Not a penalty imposed by the politician
nor the fault of comrades—
Cruelties perpetrated by me
upon my wild, passionate heart

I am enchained in a prison:
the path that leads to the beloved
There are no other handcuffs on me nor any
    fetters on my legs
A declaration of love is an act of duress, really
The promise of fidelity in love:
a hand trapped under a block of stone

Note: The lines in italics are a well-known sher by Ghalib.

29

Ghazal

How Can Friends and Comrades Gather in Celebration?

How can friends and comrades gather in celebration?
All the bottles and glasses of wine are
extinguished
How can the night of the loved ones be put together?
It's early evening and yet the hearts are
extinguished

The street of the idol-beloveds is so utterly dark
no lamp of a face, no candle of a promise
Fetch at least a faint ray of yearning
because all doors and balconies are
extinguished

I took much care to protect the promise of love, but
there have been such torrential rains this time
Every vow is erased, all messages are
extinguished

Moon of the night of sorrow, approach near
the eyes can't discern at this time at all
Whose impressions remain on the heart, whose names are
extinguished

What use is the spring's advent now? The life and soul of
the celebration of colour and song—the roses
incinerated on the bough, the entrapped hearts—are
extinguished

30

Ghazal
The Sick Are Almost Lifeless Now

The sick are almost lifeless now
Why don't you heal their malady?
What kind of a messiah are you?
Why don't you provide a cure?

Why don't you give recompense
for the pain of the night of disunion?
You shed the crazed heart's blood
Why don't you give requital?

Will you deliver justice after humanity has perished?

If you are the just judge
Why don't you now declare doomsday?

Come, you wise and subtle people
Bring lips and hearts to witness
And, O melody makers
Why are your instruments silent?

For how long will the vow of madness mortify your hands?
You, if you are true of heart
Why don't you guide them to your collars?

To have your heart laid waste is not
an obligation to discharge, O Faiz
If she is your life's torment
Why don't you forget her?

31

Life

Queen of the City of Life
how could I ever thank you?
The heart's wealth is immeasurable
why complain of being in want?

Those who forsook the world for your beauty
why should they worry about livelihood?
Marketing pain, singing melodies
what better occupation could there be?

The wine overflowed the glass
our assembly is set
who has the need to seek others' favours

to share our pain?
It takes just a teardrop for a garden to bloom
who bothers to grieve
for the tight-fistedness of the spring?

I sit happy: the desire of the eye and of the heart
is not to be found in mosque or temple
Where should I go try my luck?
all the beauty idols are seated secure in their pavilions

Who is there rich enough
with whom one could bargain
about the gold of the sun and the moon?
Let him who's keen to do battle with us
Go subdue the universe first

Note: The line in italics is by Ghalib; Faiz has used it here in a slightly ironical way.

32

Ghazal

The Sorrow of Your Love Needed Lives

The sorrow of your love needed lives
those who loved you more than life itself, they
offered themselves
There was a demand for heads in your street, so they
came out on the street

The night of waiting departed, defeated
repulsed by your perverse, unfriendly ways
Annoyed with the way I locked my state in my heart
they went away, those who would share my grief

Petitioning to meet, giving words to pain
making casual converse, protesting against hardship
My unhappy heart lost all its rights in your time

It was none other, it was us on whose dress
blackness was written openly in the streets
Those were the stains with which we adorned our bodies
before we went into the beloved's assembly

Madness for fidelity's face is no more
What will you now do with the hanging
     rope and the gallows?
The sinners who were proud of the crime
     of love are no more

33

The Rain of Stones Has Stopped

Quite unexpectedly today the sun and the moon
were disconnected from my line of sight
And smashed to bits on the horizon
There won't be any darkness or light in any
    direction now
Love's road is silent like the heart after I'm gone
What will happen now to the caravan of pain, my friends?

Let someone else now tend to the garden
of struggle and pain
Friends, the wet eye's dew is exhausted
The storm of passion is abated, the rain of stones
    has ceased

Again, the dust of the road has a tinge of the beloved's lips
My blood, like a flag, unfurls itself again
on the path to the beloved
Let's see who now is called upon when I'm no more
Is there any other who can take the man-destroying
wine of love?
The saaqi calls again and again, after I am gone

Note: The lines in italics are by Ghalib, inserted in the original
Urdu by Faiz to conclude his poem.

34

The Colours of My Heart

Before you had come, everything was just what it is now
The sky endless, the road a road
    the wine glass a wine glass
And now: wine glass, road, the sky's hue
Have all become the colour of my heart
until the liver's crushed into blood
The colour of the *champak* flower
and occasionally the hue of the joy of seeing you
Occasionally the steel grey that's the shade
of tedium
The colour of yellowed leaves, of brambles and twigs
Crimson red flowers, the colour of a flaming garden
The colour of poison, of blood and of the black night

Sky, road, wine glass
The soaked hem of a garment, a throbbing nerve
A looking glass constantly changing

Now that you have come, stay
so that some colour, some season, some entity
Should stay in place
One more time everything become just what it really is
The sky endless, the road a road
    the wine glass a wine glass

Note: The phrase in italics is by Ghalib.

35

Stay Close, Close to Me

Stay close, close to me
My slayer, keeper of my heart, stay close to me
When the night's hour flows
The dark night, drunk on the blood of the heavens
Bearing the unguent of musk and a diamond lancet
Wailing loudly, laughing and singing it goes
Clinking her purplish anklets of pain
The hour when hearts which have sunk deep into bosoms
Begin their wait for the hands that lie hidden within
    the sleeves
Hands, full of hope
When the sound of gurgling wine
begins to sound like sobbing and wailing children

Not to be placated any way at all
When nothing seems to work at all
When no conversation can begin
The hour of the night flowing
The hour of the mournful, deserted, black
    night begins to flow
Stay close
My slayer, keeper of my heart, stay close to me

Note: The lines in italics have been taken from a verse by Ghalib.

36

View (2)

Road, shadows, trees, houses and doors, edges
    of the sky dome
Upon the terrace, the moon bared her breast, gently
As someone loosens the strings of her dress, slowly
Under the edge of the sky dome, the still blue
    Nile of shadows
Forming an indigo lake
In the lake floated ever so quietly the bubble of a leaf
Floated a moment, moved away, burst, softly
Very softly, the cool colour of wine, very light
Poured into my glass, slowly
The wine glass and the wine, the wine jar, the roses
    of your hands

Like the pattern of a distant dream
Formed on its own and faded, gradually

My heart repeated some word of love, softly
You said, 'Softly.'
The moon bent down and said
'Yet more softly.'

POEMS SELECTED FROM

Sar-e Waadi-e Seena

37

Observe the City from Here

Observe the city, from here
Circle within circles, the city walls stretch
Like a prison in all directions
On every street
The prisoners walk and circulate
No milestone, no destination, no way to be set free

Should someone walk a little briskly, the question
Arises in the head
Why no challenge: Halt! Who goes there?
Should someone move a hand
Fearful, imagining inquires: Why no clink of a sword?
Why no crash of arms?

Observe the city from here, there's none
In the whole teeming populace who
Can boast of gravitas, of self-possession
None who's self-aware, who has a sense of being
Young men condemned as criminals, necks bound
With ropes; every beautiful girl a serving maid
Her ears pierced by the circlet, symbol of slavery

There are some shadows shivering around some
Lights far away, but who knows
Is it an assembly of sorrow there, or
A party of tipplers, of merrymakers?
Colours, smeared over all the doors and walls
There's no way to determine from here:
Blood or flowers?

38

Ghazal
Life of the Whole World

Life of the whole world, what word did they speak that
made you flare the corner of your lips?
Look, the brave hearts have this time declared
their madness in a thousand new ways!

A thousand arrowheads piercing our throats, and that
was the time when we struck the tune of love
A thousand arrows smashing our hearts through
and that was the time when we began our dance

No avarice, no base desire, no fear, no wild
    imaginings of danger

the head in one hand, the liver in the other
That's how, at the time of departure from the
    beloved's street, we
cast our eye on the proud and coquettish balcony

The earth in which we were pounded to dust became
the kohl for all the world's eyes
The thorn on which we sprinkled our blood, we
dyed so as to match the colour of the haughty red rose

Listen! Do you hear? The moment of union is now!
Once again at the command, 'Attend!'
We shut the casements that are the eyes and open wide
the portal of the breast

39

Wall of Night

Wall of night and the reflection of the beloved's face
    before me
Blood begins again to drip from the mirror of the heart
My way of repressing myself, not letting go
dims my sight yet again
My body aches all over again, crushed
    by trampled desire

40

Compacts Made with Desire and Longing

Compacts made with desire and longing
never reached a conclusion
Brief days and nights of loving and living
never stretched into months and years

The power of seeing which would encompass
    your full beauty
could never be acquired
Means there were of looking at you but were never
    enough to ascertain how you looked

What everyone took to be a mirage was in fact
  the river of life
Only those dreams were reliable that could never
  be imagined

Your gracious favours give no solace nor my dilating
  upon my sorrows brings relief
Buried in my heart are complaints that couldn't
  graduate to grief

A friend passed the station of life
while another didn't even pass the stage of the senses
Drinking companions for a glass or two never
could descry my true state

Come, Faiz, let's kindle our hearts and resubmit
  to the beloved
The words that came to the lips but didn't rise up
  to the level of query

41

Prayer

Come, let us also raise our hands to pray
We who have forgotten the protocols of prayer
We who don't remember anything
No God, no idol, nothing except the burning
   pain of love

Come, let us pray
that the beloved called Life may pour
tomorrow's sweetness in the poison of today
Lighten the burden of the days and nights
on the eyelashes of those
who don't have the strength any more to bear it

Brighten with a candle, any candle
The nights of those whose eyes have lost the power
to sustain the glance of morning's bright face
Bring to light a path, any path
Before the eyes of those whose feet haven't the support
of any kind of road

For those whose dogma has been to walk the path
of untruth, of hypocrisy: let them be vouchsafed
the strength of denial and intrepid search for the truth
Let those whose heads await the executioner's sword
be granted the puissant grace to wrench and spurn
the murderer's hand

The buried secret of love, which is like a fever in the spirit
Let's confess to it today and obliterate the burning pain.
The True Word, which throbs in the heart like a thorn
Let us say it today
and take away the stab of the pain

42

Ghazal
It Would Be Impossible

It would be impossible to narrate in full
the heartlessness of the times
This time around too it wasn't possible to feast
the heart to the full

Again the same promise that couldn't turn into a vow,
Again that same word, which couldn't become
positive agreement

Again the same moths, who weren't permitted
     martyrdom at the flame
Again those candles which didn't reach the night

Again that feeling of life about to expire from the lips
before the life-giving taste of the wine
Again that same assembly which couldn't grow
into a full wine-house

Again, the moment of meeting
but the eye and the power of sight thirsty for a look again
Again, the night of union: but there was no meeting
Nothing face-to-face

Again, as usual, one never knew when the door
was closed to efficacy of prayer
And again the supplication—prayer didn't come to its end

Faiz, there was doomsday's perdition here every day
And not one of those days could become the day
        of retribution

POEMS SELECTED FROM

Shaam-e Shahr-e Yaaraan

43

The Day of Death

How will it come—the day death comes?
Perhaps in the way of the bestowal of
    an undemanded kiss
On the mouth on the night of union?
The way the doors of magic lands begin to open all around
And somewhere far, the spring tide of strange,
    unknown roses
Starts suddenly to hurt the moon's breast?

Or perhaps the way
Towards the end of the night, morning made verdant by
half-open buds
Suddenly starts to ripple in the beloved's bedroom

And a jingling sound thrills the wires
through silent casements at the time of parting?

How will it come—the day death comes?
Perhaps the way a blood vessel touched by the point
of a spear shrieks out as it imagines the pain to come
And the vague shadow of the spear-handed pirate
Begins to roll and wave over the earth
from end to end?

Whichever way death comes, the day it comes
In a murderer's form, or with the elegance of a beloved
The heart will utter only these words of farewell:
Praise be to God for the end earned by the heart-stricken
And a word of thanks for the lips of the sweet-tongued!

44

An Evening in Ashkabad

When the sun, as it left
The blue horizon of Ashkabad
Poured in his golden goblet
The first red of the evening
And placing that goblet before you
Spoke to you thus:
'Salutations!
Arise
And arising from the flower bed of your body
This evening, print
A message of sweetness
To someone's name
On the lip of the goblet.'

You perhaps consented and then
You made a gift of your rosy lips
To someone
On the lip of the goblet
Or perhaps
You, bedecked on the flower bed of your body
Were so lost in you repose
That the goblet lamp
Vainly waited for you
And its light went out
Across the blue horizon of Ashkabad
An evening laid to waste

45

If My Pain Was Given Words

My pain, soundless music
My being, a nameless atom
If my pain was given words
I would know my name, my whereabouts
If I were to get a clue to my being
I would know the secret of what makes the world go round
And if I were to plumb that secret
My silence would be granted utterance
I would be lord of the universe
I would gain the riches of the two worlds

46

Evening, Be Gracious

Evening, be gracious
Evening of the city of friends
Be gracious upon us
Hell-born noontide of tyranny
Of tyranny without cause
Noontide of pain and rage and sorrow
Of tongueless pain and rage and sorrow
Whiplashes of the hell-born noontide
Rainbow-hued, map the bodies, dividing them
In a criss-cross of arcs
The wounds are wide open
Whose scars were thought to have faded
Surely there must be something in your satchel

Spread the gentle shawl of a pain-curing salve
Over that part of the body that hurts the most
Evening, be gracious
Evening of the city of friends
Be gracious upon us

Hellish deserts of hatred
Of heartless hatreds
Shards from the eye of the jealous
Shrivelled-up sward and straw of ill will
The roads so deserted
The execution halls so densely full
Through which we have passed
Every step a new blister
Our legs are slashed so
That our paths are now shrunk
Please spread under our feet
The velvet of your clouds
Cure the travellers' affliction
Evening, be gracious

O moon of the beloveds' nights
O friend and companion to the wounded hearts

Talk to us please, this evening!
Evening, be gracious
Evening, be gracious
Evening of the city of friends
Be gracious upon us

47

Ghazal
No Rivals, No Counsellors,
No Sharers of Grief

No rivals, no counsellors, no sharers of grief
How plentiful and how varied were our friends
when you and I were lovers

How many were the kinds of nearness we enjoyed
   when we weren't together—
And how many are the kinds of distance there are
   when we are together!

Arrived at your doorstep, how esteemed and
   creditworthy I became—

Yet how many were the jeers of disreputation that I earned along the journey!

It's just because of the submissive, humble ways of the simple-hearted fellows like me
How much and how often have the false idols lorded it over the whole world!

Sometimes I feel happy being oppressed and sometimes I'm unhappy at grace and kindness
How many ways you taught me of being cross or perverse!

48

After a Visit to Dhaka

So, we were determined to be strangers—after so much
Affability, conviviality
How many meetings would be needed
to be declared familiar friends?

When will the springtime of spotless verdure be?
How many seasons of rain will it take to wash off
the stains of blood?

They were extremely cruel
those moments of the ceasing of the pain of love
They were extremely cold and loveless the mornings
that followed the gentle loving nights

The heart was keen enough, but its breaking gave
    no respite
For me to submit a few plaints and reproaches after
the entreaties were over

Prepared to give away my life for her, I approached her with
the idea of saying something meaningful
Unfortunately those very words remained unsaid
    after I'd said
all that I wanted to say

49

Do What You Must Do

Now why talk of the day
When the heart will be shattered
And all kinds of sorrow will be no more
Whatever was gained would be lost
And we'll get what we never could get?
This day is that very first day—
The first day of love
The day we always longed for
And whose advent we always dreaded
Numerous are the times when this day came
We were settled a hundred times, plundered
    a hundred times
Sacked, and compensated a hundred times

Why worry now about the day
When the heart will be shattered
And all kinds of sorrow will be no more?
Pass by anxious thoughts and fears
Que sera sera—
If it's to be laughter, then laughter it'll be
If it's to be tears, then tears it'll be
Do what you must do
Whatever happens, we'll see how it goes

50

I Spent Some of My Time Loving, Some of My Time Working

Those guys were truly lucky
Who regarded loving as a full-time job
Or used their loving for their job
Throughout my life, I was busy
I spent some of my time loving, some of my time working
My work impeded my loving all the time
And my loving ravelled my work
So then finally fed up with both
I came away with both unfinished

51

Imagination Again Seeks a Word

(1)

Imagination again seeks a word everywhere, today
A honey-filled word, a vitriol-filled word
A word that finds its target in the heart
A word full of destructive fury
Word of love, like a loving, heart-consoling glance
Which meets the eyes like a kiss on the lips
Bright like the head of a golden wave
Like the opening of the time of pleasure and song
in a lover's company
Word of abomination, like the sword of wrath
That would destroy the cities of tyranny until eternity
without end

Dark as night on a burning ghat
It would blacken my lips if I were to utter that word

(2)
All connections break today between all notes and all ragas
Once again the voice searches for the singer it has lost
The fury of pain has ripped into shreds, like Majnun's collar
Each and every thread in each and every wire
of every musical instrument
Today, all people, all creation demands from every wave
    of wind
May you live long, bring to us a song, a sound!
Let it be a keening in sorrow, or the tumult of martyrdom
Or the last trump, or doomsday's thunder

POEMS SELECTED FROM

Mere Dil Mere Musaafir

52

My Heart, O My Wayfarer!

My heart, O my wayfarer
The command has been given again
The two of us should be banished from the homeland
And wander from street to street, calling
Travel from one city to the next
Hoping to find some trace, or clue
To a loving courier
Ask every stranger
The address where we used to live
Around the streets and dwellings of strangers
We should drag the day to night—
Picking up conversations
With this or that individual[1]

What can I tell you what it is?
The night of affliction and sorrow is a calamitous thing!
We could even make do with it
Were there a count, a limit
It's never too bad to die
If it's only once [2]

---

[1] This recalls a verse by Mushafi, the classical Urdu poet, contemporary of Mir.

[2] These lines echo a verse from a famous ghazal by Ghalib.

53

View (3)

The sky is a turbulent sea today
Cloud-ships moving about everywhere on it
On their decks masts of the sun's rays
Wearing the long, heavy coats of the sails
Numerous dome-like islands on the Nile of the sky
And all absorbed in some sport or other
A swallow dips and bathes
A kite dives headlong—
No power testing its strength against another
No fleet displaying a country's flag
No submarines in its depths anywhere

No rockets, no naval guns here
Though all elements display their might here
Yet how peaceful is this turbulent sea

54

A Ghazal for the Hafiz of Shiraz

The counsellor said to me, 'What merit does love have
except sorrow?'
Go away, wise master. Is there any better merit?

(Hafiz)

Candy of the mouth—just a little more
Pleasure and elegance in poetry—just a little more

Joys of the spring in the season of the fall
Jasmine petals—just a little more

Bitter song on the plight of the garden
Bird of the garden—just a little more

Breaking the heart, giving it solace
Remembrance of home—just a little more

The body's lamp, dressed as a lampshade
The body's beauty—just a little more

What does love have but sorrow?
My masters—just a little more

55

Ghazal

Tyranny Giving Lessons in the Fidelity of Love

Tyranny giving lessons in the fidelity of love?
That's not how things happen
False idols leading the way to the true God?
That's not how things happen

Take into account also the desires that were slaughtered
    in the body's execution house
Dear murderer, computing the blood money?
That's not how these things happen

Stratagems, penalties, nothing works in the world
    of the heart
Vow of submission, promise to always subserve?
That's not how these things happen here

Doomsday's tumult happening every night, every
    pass of the night—
Such things can be, but
With every morning should dawn the day
of reward or retribution—
No, that's not how things happen

Well, the time's pulse still beats, the heavens all
    rotate as before
And you say: Everything has come to pass, but
That's not how things happen

POEMS SELECTED FROM

Ghubaar-e Ayyaam

56

Ash of Disunion, Blossoms of Union

Today, once again in the thread of pain and grief
I thread the blossoms of your memory

Picking from the wasteland of the act of
renunciation of love
Flowers of the months and years of loving

I adorned your doorstep with them, again
And made a sacred offering

Ash of disunion, blossoms of union
Tied in the hem of desire

57

Homage to Maulana Hasrat Mohani

They will die but will never support the tyrant
The free will never give up their tradition

What an embarrassment of riches we had when
    once we met!
Now there'll never be complaining against your
    not meeting me

So the night is past, the day too shall pass
I'll not speak of whatever befell, moment from moment

Poverty is enough recompense for my melancholy heart
I won't demand a kingdom, I won't rule a dominion

I am neither the sheikh, nor leader, nor courtier, nor journalist
I'll not preach what I don't practise

Appendix

Urdu Transliteration of the Poems

1. Ek Manzar (1)

Baam-o dar khamoshi ke bojh se choor
Aasmaanon se ju-e dard rawaan
Chaand ka dukh bhara fasaana-e noor
Shahraahon ki khaak mein ghaltaan
Khwaabgaahon mein neem taareeki
Muzmahil lai rubaab-e hasti ki
Halke halke suron mein nauha kunaan

~

2. Mujhse Pehli Si Muhabbat Meri Mehboob Na Maang

Mujhse pehli si muhabbat meri mehboob na maang
Maine samjha ki tu hai toh darakhshaan hai hayaat

Tera gham hai toh gham-e dahr ka jhagda kya hai
Teri soorat se hai aalam mein bahaaron ko sabaat
Teri aankhon ke siva duniya mein rakkha kya hai?
Tu jo mil jaaye toh taqdeer nigoon ho jaaye
Yun na tha maine faqat chaaha tha yun ho jaaye
Aur bhi dukh hain zamaane mein muhabbat ke siva
Raahatein aur bhi hain wasl ki raahat ke siva
Anginat sadiyon ke taareek bahimaana tilism
Resham-o atlas-o kamkhwaab mein bunwaaye huwe
Ja baja koocha-o bazaar mein bikte huwe jism
Khaak mein lithde huwe khoon mein nehlaaye huwe
Laut jaati hai idhar ko bhi nazar kya kije
Ab bhi dilkash hai tera husn magar kya kije
Aur bhi dukh hain zamaane mein muhabbat ke siva
Raahatein aur bhi hain wasl ki raahat ke siva
Mujhse pehli si muhabbat meri mehboob na maang

~

3.
Donon Jahaan Teri Muhabbat Mein Haar Ke

Donon jahaan teri muhabbat mein haar ke
Woh ja raha hai koi shab-e gham guzaar ke

Veeraan hai maikada khum-o saagar udaas hain
Tum kya gaye ki rooth gaye din bahaar ke
Ik fursat-e gunaah mili woh bhi chaar din
Dekhe hain humne hausle parvardigaar ke
Duniya ne teri yaad se begaana kar diya
Tujhse bhi dil fareb hain gham rozgaar ke
Bhoole se muskura toh diye thhe woh aaj Faiz
Mat poochh valvale dil-e naakarda kaar ke

~

4. Tanhaai

Phir koi aaya dil-e zaar nahin koi nahin
Raah-rau hoga kahin aur chala jaayega
Dhal chuki raat bikharne laga taaron ka ghubaar
Ladkhadaane lage aiwaanon mein khwaabeedah charaagh
So gayi rasta tak tak ke har ik raahguzaar
Ajnabi khaak ne dhundla diye kadmon ke suraagh
Gul karo shamaein badha do mai-o mina-o ayaagh
Apne be-khwaab kiwaadon ko muqaffal kar lo
Ab yahan koi nahin koi nahin aayega

~

5. Chand Roz Aur Meri Jaan

Chand roz aur meri jaan faqat chand hi roz
Zulm ki chhaaon mein dum lene pe majboor hain hum
Aur kuchh der sitam seh lein tadap lein ro lein
Apne ajdaad ki meeraas hai maazoor hain hum
Jism par qaid hai jazbaat pe zanjeerein hain
Fikr mehboos hai guftaar pe taazeerein hain
Apni himmat hai ki hum phir bhi jiye jaate hain
Zindagi kya kisi muflis ki qaba hai jis mein
Har ghadi dard ke paiwand lage jaate hain
Lekin ab zulm ki miyaad ke din thode hain
Ek zara sabr ki fariyaad ke din thode hain

Arsa-e dahr ki jhulsi hui veeraani mein
Humko rehna hai pe yun hi toh nahin rehna hai
Ajnabi haathon ka be-naam giraanbaar sitam
Aaj sehna hai hamesha toh nahin sehna hai

Yeh tere husn se lipti hui aalaam ki gard
Apni do-roza jawaani ki shikaston ka shumaar
Chaandni raaton ka bekaar dehekta hua dard

Dil ki be-soodh tadap jism ki maayoos pukaar
Chand roz aur meri jaan faqat chand hi roz

~

6. Marg-e Soz-e Muhabbat

Aao ki marg-e soz-e muhabbat manaayein hu
Aao ki husn-e maah se dil ko jalaayein hum
Khush hon firaaq-e qaamat-o rukhsaar-e yaar se
Sarv-o gul-o saman se nazar ko sataayein hum
Veeraani-e hayaat ko veeraan tar karein
Le naaseh aaj tera kaha maan jaayein hum
Phir ot leke daaman-e abr-e bahaar ki
Dil ko manaayein hum kabhi aansu bahaayein hum
Suljhaayein be-dili se yeh uljhe huwe sawaal
Wahan jaayein ya na jaayein na jaayein ki jaayein hum
Phir dil ko paas-e zabt ki talqeen kar chukein
Aur imtehaan-e zabt se phir ji churaayein hum
Aao ki aaj khatm hui daastaan-e ishq
Ab khatm-e aashiqi ke fasaane sunaayein hum

~

7. Bol

Bol ki lab azaad hain tere
Bol zabaan ab tak teri hai
Tera sutvaan jism hai tera
Bol ki jaan ab tak teri hai
Dekh ki aahan-gar ki dukaan mein
Tund hain shole surkh hai aahan
Khulne lage quflon ke dahaane
Phaila har ik zanjeer ka daaman
Bol yeh thoda waqt bahut hai
Jism-o zabaan ki maut se pehle
Bol ki sach zinda hai ab tak
Bol jo kuchh kehna hai keh le

~

8. Iqbal

Aaya hamaare des mein ik khush-nawa faqir
Aaya aur apni dhun mein ghazal-khwaan guzar gaya
Sunsaan raahein khalq se aabaad ho gayin
Veeraan maikadon ka naseeba sanvar gaya
Thiin chand hi nigaahein jo uss tak pahunch sakin
Par uska geet sabke dilon mein utar gaya

Ab door ja chuka hai woh shah-e gada-numa
Aur phir se apne des ki raahein udaas hain
Chand ik ko yaad hai koi uski ada-e khaas
Do ik nigaahein chand azeezon ke paas hain
Par uska geet sabke dilon mein muqeem hai
Aur uski lai se sainkdon lazzat shanaas hain

Uss geet ke tamaam muhaasin hain la-zavaal
Uska vafoor uska kharosh uska soz-o saaz
Yeh geet misl-e shola-e javvaala tund-o tez
Uski lapak se baad-e fana ka jigar gudaaz
Jaise charaagh vahshat-e sar sar se be-khatar
Ya shamm-e bazm subh ki aamad se be-khabar

~

9. Shahraah

Ek afsurda shahraah hai daraaz
Door ufuq par nazar jamaaye huwe
Sard mitti pe apne seene ke
Surmagin husn ko bichhaaye huwe

Jis tarah koi gham-zada aurat
Apne veeraankade mein mahv-e khayaal
Wasl-e mehboob ke tasavvur mein
Mu ba mu choor uzv uzv nidhaal

~

10. Nazm
Mata-e Lauh-o Qalam

Mata-e lauh-o qalam chhin gai toh kya gham hai
Ki khoon-e dil mein dubo li hain ungliyaan maine
Zabaan pe mohr lagi hai toh kya ki rakh di hai
Har ek halqa-e zanjeer mein zabaan maine

~

11. Mere Humdum Mere Dost

Gar mujhe iska yaqeen ho mere humdum mere dost
Gar mujhe iska yaqeen ho ki tere dil ki thakan
Teri aankhon ki udaasi tere seene ki jalan

Meri diljooi mere pyaar se mit jaayegi
Gar mera harf-e tasalli woh dawa ho jis se
Ji uthe phir tera ujda hua be-noor dimaagh
Teri peshaani se dhul jaayein yeh tazleel ke daagh
Teri bimaar jawaani ko shifa ho jaaye
Gar mujhe iska yaqeen ho mere humdum mere dost
Roz-o shab shaam-o seher main tujhe behlaata rahun
Main tujhe geet sunaata rahun halke sheereen
Aabshaaron ke bahaaron ke chaman zaaron ke geet
Aamad-e subh ke mehtaab ke sayyaaron ke geet
Tujhse main husn-o muhabbat ki hikayaat kahun
Kaise maghroor hasinaon ke barfaab se jism
Garm haathon ki haraarat mein pighal jaate hain
Kaise ik chehre ke thehre huwe maanoos naqoosh
Dekhte dekhte yak-lakht badal jaate hain
Kis tarah aariz-e mehboob ka shaffaaf billoor
Yak-bayak baada-e ahmar se dahak jaata hai
Kaise gulchhin ke liye jhukti hai khud shaakh-e gulaab
Kis tarah raat ka aiwaan mehak jaata hai
Yun hi gaata rahun gaata rahun teri khaatir
Geet bunta rahun baitha rahun teri khaatir
Par mere geet tere dukh ka mudaawa hi nahin
Naghma jarraah nahin mooniis-o ghamkhwaar sahi

Geet nashtar toh nahin marham-e aazaar sahi
Tere aazaar ka chaara nahin nashtar ke siva
Aur yeh saffaak maseeha mere qabze mein nahin
Iss jahaan ke kisi zi-rooh ke qabze mein nahin
Haan magar tere siva tere siva tere siva

~

12. Subh-e Azaadi

Yeh daagh daagh ujaala yeh shab-gazeda seher
Woh intezaar tha jiska yeh woh seher toh nahin
Yeh woh seher toh nahin jiski aarzu le kar
Chale thhe yaar ki mil jaayegi kahin na kahin
Falak ke dasht mein taaron ki aakhri manzil
Kahin toh hoga shab-e sust mauj ka saahil
Kahin toh jaake rukega safeena-e gham-e dil

Jawaan lahu ki pur asraar shahraahon se
Chale jo yaar toh daaman pe kitne haath pade
Dayaar-e husn ki be-sabr khwaabgaahon se
Pukaarti rahin baahein badan bulaate rahe
Bahut azeez thi lekin rukh-e seher ki lagan

Bahut qareen tha haseena-e noor ka daaman
Subuk subuk thi tamanna dabi dabi thi thakan

Suna hai ho bhi chuka hai firaaq-e zulmat-o noor
Suna hai ho bhi chuka hai wisaal-e manzil-o gaam
Badal chuka hai bahut ahl-e dard ka dastoor
Nishaat-e wasl halaal-o azaab-e hijr haraam

Jigar ki aag nazar ki umang dil ki jalan
Kisi pe chaara-e hijraan ka kuchh asar hi nahin
Kahan se aayi nigaar-e saba kidhar ko gayi
Abhi charaagh-e sar-e rah ko kuchh khabar hi nahin
Abhi giraani-e shab mein kami nahin aayi
Najaat-e deeda-o dil ki ghadi nahin aayi
Chale chalo ki woh manzil abhi nahin aayi

~

13. Lauh-o Qalam

Hum parvarish-e lauh-o qalam karte rahenge
Jo dil pe guzarti hai raqam karte rahenge
Asbaab-e gham-e ishq baham karte rahenge

Veeraani-e dauraan pe karam karte rahenge
Haan talkhi-e ayyaam abhi aur badhegi
Haan ahl-e sitam mashq-e sitam karte rahenge
Manzoor yeh talkhi yeh sitam humko gawaara
Dum hai toh mudaawa-e alam karte rahenge
Maikhaana salaamat hai toh hum surkhi-e mai se
Taz-in-e dar-o baam-e haram karte rahenge
Baaki hai lahu dil mein toh har ashk se paida
Rang-e lab-o rukhsaar-e sanam karte rahenge
Ik tarz-e taghaaful hai so woh unko mubaarak
Ik arz-e tamanna hai so hum karte rahenge

~

14. Tumhaari Yaad Ke Jab Zakhm Bharne Lagte Hain

Tumhaari yaad ke jab zakhm bharne lagte hain
Kisi bahaane tumhein yaad karne lagte hain
Hadees-e yaar ke unvaan nikharne lagte hain
Toh har hareem mein gesu sanvarne lagte hain
Har ajnabi humein mehram dikhaayi deta hai
Jo ab bhi teri gali se guzarne lagte hain

Saba se karte hain ghurbat naseeb zikr-e vatan
Toh chashm-e subh mein aansu ubharne lagte hain
Woh jab bhi karte hain iss nutq-o lab ki bakhiya-gari
Fiza mein aur bhi naghme bikharne lagte hain
Dar-e qafas pe andhere ki mohr lagti hai
Toh Faiz dil mein sitaare utarne lagte hain

~

15. Tumhaare Husn Ke Naam

Salaam likhta hai shaayar tumhaare husn ke naam
Bikhar gaya jo kabhi rang-e pairahan sar-e baam
Nikhar gayi hai kabhi subh dopahr kabhi shaam
Kahin jo qaamat-e zeba pe saj gayi hai qaba
Chaman mein sarv-o sanobar sanwar gaye hain tamaam
Bani bisaat-e ghazal jab dubo liye dil ne
Tumhaare saaya-e rukhsaar-o lab mein saagar-o jaam
Salaam likhta hai shaayar tumhaare husn ke naam

Tumhaare haath pe hai taabish-e hina jab tak
Jahaan mein baaki hai dildaari-e uroos-e sukhan
Tumhaara husn jawaan hai toh mehrbaan hai falak
Tumhaara dum hai toh dumsaaz hai hawa-e watan

Agarche tang hain auqaat sakht hain aalaam
Tumhaari yaad se sheereen hai talkhi-e ayyaam
Salaam likhta hai shaayar tumhaare husn ke naam

~

16. Rang Pairaahan Ka Khushbu Zulf Lehraane Ka Naam

Rang pairaahan ka khushbu zulf lehraane ka naam
Mausam-e gul hai tumhaare baam par aane ka naam
Doston uss chashm-o lab ki kuchh kaho jiske baghair
Gulsitaan ki baat rangeen hai na maikhaane ka naam
Phir nazar mein phool mehke dil mein phir shammein jalin

~

17. Dil Mein Ab Yun Tere Bhoole Huwe Gham Aate Hain

Dil mein ab yun tere bhoole huwe gham aate hain
Jaise bichhde huwe kaabe mein sanam aate hain

Ek ek karke huwe jaate hain taare raushan
Meri manzil ki taraf tere qadam aate hain
Raqs-e mai tez karo saaz ki lai tez karo
Su-e maikhaana safeeraan-e haram aate hain
Kuchh humin ko nahin ehsaan uthaane ka dimaagh
Woh toh jab aate hain ma'il ba-karam aate hain
Aur kuchh der na guzre shab-e furqat se kaho
Dil bhi kam dukhta hai woh yaad bhi kam aate hain

~

18. Sheeshon Ka Maseeha Koi Nahin

Moti ho ki sheesha jaam ki dur
Jo toot gaya so toot gaya
Kab ashkon se jud sakta hai
Jo toot gaya so chhoot gaya

Tum naahaq tukde chun chun kar
Daaman mein chhipaaye baithe ho
Sheeshon ka maseeha koi nahin
Kya aas lagaaye baithe ho

Shaayad ki inhin tukdon mein kahin
Woh saagar-e dil hai jis mein kabhi
Sad naaz se utra karti thi
Sahba-e gham-e jaanaan ki pari

Phir duniya waalon ne tumse
Yeh saagar le kar phod diya
Jo mai thi baha di mitti mein
Mehmaan ka shahpar tod diya

Yeh rangeen reze hain shaayad
Un shokh bilori sapnon ke
Tum mast jawaani mein jin se
Khalwat ko sajaaya karte thhe

Naadaari daftar bhookh aur gham
In sapnon se takraate rahe
Be-raham tha chaumukh pathrao
Yeh kaanch ke dhaanche kya karte

Ya shaayad in zarron mein kahin
Moti hai tumhaari izzat ka

Woh jis se tumhaare ijz pe bhi
Shamshaad qadon ne rashk kiya

Iss maal ki dhun mein phirte thhe
Taajir bhi bahut rahzan bhi kayi
Hai chor nagar yaan muflis ki
Gar jaan bachi toh aan gayi

Yeh saagar sheeshe laal-o guhar
Saalim hon toh qeemat paate hain
Yun tukde tukde hon toh faqat
Chubhte hain lahu rulvaate hain

Tum naahaq sheeshe chun chun kar
Daaman mein chhipaaye baithe ho
Sheeshon ka maseeha koi nahin
Kya aas lagaaye baithe ho

Yaadon ke girebaanon ke rafu
Par dil ki guzar kab hoti hai
Ek bakhiya udhera ek siya
Yun umr basar kab hoti hai

Iss kaar gah-e hasti mein jahan
Yeh saagar sheeshe dhalte hain
Har shai ka badal mil sakta hai
Sab daaman pur ho sakte hain

Jo haath badhe yaawar hai yahan
Jo aankh uthe woh bakhtaawar
Yahan dhan daulat ka ant nahin
Hon ghaat mein daaku laakh magar

Kab loot jhapat se hasti ki
Dukaanein khaali hoti hain
Yahan parbat parbat heere hain
Yahan saagar saagar moti hain

Kuchh log hain jo iss daulat par
Parde latkaate phirte hain
Har parbat ko har saagar ko
Neelaam chadhaate phirte hain

Kuchh woh bhi hain jo lad bhid kar
Yeh parde noch giraate hain
Hasti ke uthai geeron ki
Har chaal uljhaaye jaate hain

In donon mein rann padta hai
Nit basti basti nagar nagar
Har baste ghar ke seene mein
Har chalti raah ke maathe par

Yeh kaalik bharte phirte hain
Woh jot jaagate rehte hain
Yeh aag lagaate phirte hain
Woh aag bujhaate rehte hain

Sab saagar sheeshe laal-o guhar
Iss baazi mein badd jaate hain
Uthao sab khaali haathon ko
Iss rann se bulaave aate hain

~

19. Aaye Kuchh Abr Kuchh Sharaab Aaye

Aaye kuchh abr kuchh sharaab aaye
Iske baad aaye jo azaab aaye
Baam-e meena se mahtaab utre
Dast-e saaqi mein aftaab aaye
Har rag-e khoon mein phir charaaghan ho

Saamne phir woh be-naqaab aaye
Umr ke har varq pe dil ko nazar
Teri mehr-o wafa ke baab aaye
Kar raha tha gham-e jahaan ka hisaab
Aaj tum yaad be-hisaab aaye
Na gayi tere gham ki sardaari
Dil mein yun roz inqilaab aaye
Jal uthe bazm-e ghair ke dar-o baam
Jab bhi hum khaanumaan kharaab aaye
Iss tarah apni khamoshi goonji
Goya har simt se jawaab aaye
Faiz thi raah sar basar manzil
Hum jahan pahunche kaamiyaab aaye

~

20. Zindaan Ki Ek Shaam

Shaam ke pech-o kham sitaaron se
Zeena zeena utar rahi hai raat
Yun saba paas se guzarti hai
Jaise keh di kisi ne pyaar ki baat
Sehn-e zindaan ke be-watan ashjaar

Sar nigun mahv hain banaane mein
Daaman-e aasmaan pe naqsh-o nigaar
Shaana-e baam par damakta hai
Meherbaan chaandni ka dast-e jameel
Khaak mein ghul gayi hai aab-e nujoom
Noor mein ghul gaya hai arsh ka neel
Sabz goshon mein neelgoon saaye
Lahlahaate hain jis tarah dil mein
Mauj-e dard-e firaaq-e yaar aaye

Dil se paiham khayaal kehta hai
Itni sheereen hai zindagi iss pal
Zulm ka zahr gholne waale
Kaamraan ho sakenge aaj na kal
Jalva gaah-e wisaal ki shamaein
Woh bujha bhi chuke agar toh kya
Chaand ko gul karein toh hum jaanein

~

21. Zindaan Ki Ek Subh

Raat baaki thi abhi jab sar-e baaleen aakar
Chaand ne mujhse kaha

Jaag seher aayi hai
Jaag iss shab jo mai-e khwaab tera hissa thi
Jaam ke lab se tah-e jaam utar aayi hai
Aks-e jaanaan ko vida karke uthi meri nazar
Shab ke thehre huwe paani ki siyah chaadar par
Ja ba ja raqs mein aane lage chaandi ke bhanwar
Chaand ke haath se taaron ke kanwal gir gir kar
Doobte tairte murjhaate rahe khilte rahe
Raat aur subh bahut der gale milte rahe

Sehn-e zindaan mein rafeeqon ke sunehre chehre
Sath-e zulmat se damakte huwe ubhre kam kam
Neend ki os ne unn chehron se dho daala tha
Des ka dard firaaq-e rukh-e mehboob ka gham

Door naubat hui phirne lage bezaar qadam
Zard faaqon ke sataaye huwe pehre waale
Ahl-e zindaan ke ghazabnaak kharoshaan naale
Jinki baahon mein phira karte hain baahein daale

Lazzat-e khwaab se makhmoor hawaein jaagin
Jail ki zahr bhari choor sadaein jaagin
Door darwaaza khula koi koi band hua

Door machli koi zanjeer machal ke royi
Door utra kisi taale ke jigar mein khanjar

Sar patakne laga reh reh ke dareecha koi
Goya phir khwaab se bedaar huwe dushman-e jaan
Sang-o faulaad se dhaale huwe jinnaat-e giraan
Jinke changul mein shab-o roz hain fariyaad kunaan
Mere bekaar shab-o roz ki naazuk pariyaan
Apne shahpoor ki raah dekh rahi hain yeh aseer
Jiske tarkash mein hain ummeed ke jalte huwe teer
                                        (Na tamaam)

~

22. Yaad

Dasht-e tanhaai mein ay jaan-e jahaan larzaan hain
Teri aawaaz ke saaye tere honton ke saraab
Dasht-e tanhaai mein doori ke khas-o khaak taley
Khil rahe hain tere pahlu ke saman aur gulaab

Uth rahi hai kahin qurbat se teri saans ki aanch
Apni khushbu mein sulagti hui maddham maddham

Door ufaq paar chamakti hui qatra qatra
Gir rahi hai teri dildaar nazar ki shabnam

Iss qadar pyaar se ay jaan-e jahaan rakkha hai
Dil ke rukhsaar pe iss waqt teri yaad ne haath
Yun gumaan hota hai garche hai abhi subh-e firaaq
Dhal gaya hijr ka din aa bhi gayi wasl ki raat

~

23. Mulaqaat

(1)
Yeh raat uss dard ka shajar hai
Jo mujhse tujhse azeem tar hai
Azeem tar hai ki iss ki shaakhon
Mein laakh mashal bakaf sitaaron
Ke kaarwaan ghir ke kho gaye hain
Hazaar mehtaab iske saaye
Mein apna sab noor ro gaye hain

Yeh raat uss dard ka shajar hai
Jo mujhse tujhse azeem tar hai

Magar issi raat ke shajar se
Yeh chand lamhon ke zard patte

Gire hain aur tere gesuon mein
Ulajh ke gulnaar ho gaye hain
Issi ki shabnam se khamoshi ke
Yeh chand qatre teri jabeen par
Baras ke heere piro gaye hain

(2)
Bahut siyah hai yeh raat lekin
Issi siyaahi mein roonuma hai
Woh nahr-e khoon jo meri sada hai
Issi ke saaye mein noor gar hai
Woh mauj-e zar jo teri nazar hai

Woh gham jo iss waqt teri baahon
Ke gulsitaan mein sulag raha hai
(Woh gham jo iss raat ka samar hai)
Kuchh aur tap jaaye apni aahon
Ki aanch mein toh yehi sharar hai

Har ik siyah shaakh ki kamaan se
Jigar mein toote hain teer jitne

Jigar se noche hain aur har ik
Ka humne teesha bana liya hai

(3)
Alam naseebon jigar figaaron
Ki subh aflaak par nahin hai
Jahan pe hum tum khade hain donon
Seher ka raushan ufuq yahin hai
Yahin pe gham ke sharaar khil kar
Shafaq ka gulzaar ban gaye hain
Yahin pe qaatil dukhon ke teeshe
Qataar andar qataar kirnon
Ke aatisheen haar ban gaye hain
Yeh gham jo iss raat ne diya hai
Yeh gham seher ka yaqeen bana hai
Yaqeen jo gham se kareem tar hai
Seher jo shab se azeem tar hai

~

24. Kab Yaad Mein Tera Saath Nahin

Kab yaad mein tera saath nahin kab haath mein tera haath
nahin
Sad shukr ki apni raaton mein ab hijr ki koi raat nahin
Mushkil hain agar haalaat wahan dil bech aayein jaan de
aayein
Dil waalon koocha-e jaanaan mein kya aise bhi haalaat
nahin
Jis dhaj se koi maqtal mein gaya woh shaan salaamat rehti
hai
Yeh jaan toh aani jaani hai iss jaan ki toh koi baat nahin
Maidaan-e wafa darbaar nahin yahan naam-o nasab ki
poochh kahan
Aashiq toh kisi ka naam nahin kuchh ishq kisi ki zaat
nahin
Gar baazi ishq ki baazi hai jo chaaho laga do dar kaisa
Gar jeet gaye toh kya kehna haare bhi toh baazi maat
nahin

~

25. Ay Raushniyon Ke Shahr

Sabza sabza sookh rahi hai pheeki zard dopahr
Deewaaron ko chaat raha hai tanhaai ka zahr
Door ufuq tak ghat-ti badhti uth-ti girti rehti hai
Kohr ki soorat be-raunaq dardon ki gadli lahr
Basta hai iss kohr ke peechhe raushniyon ka shahr

Ay raushniyon ke shahr
Kaun kahe kis simt hai teri raushniyon ki raah
Har jaanib be-noor khadi hai hijr ki shahr panaah
Thak kar har su baith rahi hai shauq ki maand sipaah
Aaj mera dil fikr mein hai
Ay raushniyon ke shahr
Shab khoon se munh pher na jaaye armaanon ki rau
Khair ho teri lailaon ki un sab se keh do
Aaj ki shab jab diye jalaayein oonchi rakkhein lau

~

26. Kuchh Mohtasibon Ki Khalwat Mein

Kuchh mohtasibon ki khalwat mein kuchh waa'iz ke ghar
    jaati hai
Hum baadakashon ke hisse ki ab jaam mein kam tar jaati hai

Yun arz-o talab se kab ay dil patthar dil paani hote hain
Tum laakh raza ki khu daalo kab khu-e sitamgar jaati hai
Bedaad garon ki basti hai yahan daad kahan khairat kahan
Sar phodti phirti hai nadaan fariyaad jo dar dar jaati hai
Haan jaan ke ziyaan ki hum ko bhi tashweesh hai lekin
    kya kije
Har rah jo udhar ko jaati hai maqtal se guzar kar jaati hai
Ab koocha-e dilbar ka rahrau rahzan bhi bane toh baat bane
Pehre se adu talte hi nahin aur raat baraabar jaati hai
Hum ahl-e qafas tanha bhi nahin har roz naseem-e
    subh-e watan
Yaadon se mu'attar aati hai ashkon se munawwar jaati hai

~

27. Koi Aashiq Kisi Mehbooba Se

Yaad ki raahguzar jis pe issi soorat se
Muddatein beet gayi hain tumhein chalte chalte
Khatm ho jaaye jo do chaar qadam aur chalo
Mod padta hai jahaan dasht-e faraamoshi ka
Jis se aage na koi main hun na koi tum ho
Saans thaame hain nigaahein ki na jaane kis dum
Tum palat aao guzar jao ya mud kar dekho

Garche waaqif hain nigaahein ki yeh sab dhokha hai
Gar kahin tumse hum-aaghosh hui phir se nazar
Phoot niklegi wahan aur koi raahguzar
Phir issi tarah jahan hoga muqaabil paiham
Saaya-e zulf ka aur jumbish-e baazu ka safar

Doosri baat bhi jhoothi hai ki dil jaanta hai
Yahan koi mod koi dasht koi ghaat nahin
Jiske parde mein mera maah-e rawaan doob sake
Tumse chalti rahe yeh raah yun hi achchha hai
Tumne mud kar bhi na dekha toh koi baat nahin

~

28. Dast-e Tah-e Sang Aamdah

Bezaar fiza dar pa-e aazaar saba hai
Yun hai ki har ik humdum-e dereena khafa hai
Haan bada kasho aaya hai ab rang pe mausam
Ab sair ke kaabil rawish-e aab-o hawa hai
Umdi hai har ik simt se ilzaam ki barsaat
Chhaayi hui har daang malaamat ki ghata hai
Woh cheez bhari hai ki sulagti hai suraahi

Har kaasa-e mai zahr-e halaahal se siwa hai
Haan jaam uthao ki ba yaad-e lab-e sheereen
Yeh zahr toh yaaron ne kayi baar piya hai
Iss jazba-e dil ki na saza hai na jaza hai
Maqsood-e rah-e shauq wafa hai na jafa hai
Ehsaas-e gham-e dil jo gham-e dil ka sila hai
Uss husn ka ehsaas hai jo teri ata hai
Har subh-e gulistaan hai tera ru-e bahaarin
Har phool teri yaad ka naqsh-e kaf-e pa hai
Har bheegi hui raat teri zulf ki shabnam
Dhalta hua sooraj tere honton ki fiza hai
Har raah pahunchti hai teri chaah ke dar tak
Har harf-e tamanna tere qadmon ki sada hai
Taazeer-e siyaasat hai na ghairon ki khata hai
Woh zulm jo humne dil-e wahshi pe kiya hai
Zindaan-e raah-e yaar mein paaband huwe hum
Zanjeer bakaf hai na koi band bapa hai
'Majboori-o daawa-e giriftaari-e ulfat
Dast-e tah-e sang aamdah paimaan-e wafa hai'

~

29. Jamegi Kaise Bisaat-e Yaaraan Ki Sheesha-o Jaam Bujh Gaye Hain

Jamegi kaise bisaat-e yaaraan ki sheesha-o jaam bujh
gaye hain

Sajegi kaise shab-e nigaaraan ki dil sar-e shaam bujh
gaye hain

Woh teergi hai raah-e butaan mein charaagh-e rukh hai
na shamm-e waada

Kiran koi aarzu ki laao ki sab dar-o baam bujh gaye hain

Bahut sambhaala wafa ka paimaan magar woh barsi hai
ab ke barkha

Har ek iqraar mit gaya hai tamaam paighaam bujh gaye hain

Kareeb ay mah-e shab-e gham nazar pe khulta nahin kuchh
iss dum

Ki dil pe kis kis ka naqsh baaki hai kaun se naam bujh
gaye hain

Bahaar ab aake kya karegi ki jin se tha jashn-e rang-o
naghma

Woh gul sar-e shaakh jal gaye hain woh dil tah-e daam
bujh gaye hain

~

30. Be-dum Huwe Bimaar Dawa
Kyun Nahin Dete

Be-dum huwe bimaar dawa kyun nahin dete
Tum achchhe maseeha ho shifa kyun nahin dete
Dard-e shab-e hijraan ki jaza kyun nahin dete
Khoon-e dil-e wahshi ka sila kyun nahin dete
Mit jaayegi makhlooq toh insaaf karoge
Munsif ho toh ab hashr utha kyun nahin dete
Haan nukta varo laao lab-o dil ki gavaahi
Haan naghma garo saaz sada kyun nahin dete
Paimaan-e junoon haathon ko sharmaayega kab tak
Dil waalon garibaan ka pata kyun nahin dete
Barbaadi-e dil jabr nahin Faiz kisi ka
Woh dushman-e jaan hai toh bhula kyun nahin dete

~

31. Zindagi

Malka-e seher-e zindagi tera shukr kis taur se ada kije
Daulat-e dil ka kuchh shumaar nahin tang dasti ka kya
    gila kije

Jo tere husn ke faqir huwe unko tashweesh-e rozgaar kahan
Dard bechenge geet gaayenge isse khush waqt kaarobaar kahan

Jaam chhalka toh jam gayi mehfil minnat-e lutf-e gham-gusaar kise
Ashk tapka toh khil gaya gulshan ranj-e kam-zarfi-e bahaar kise

Khush nasheen hain ki chashm-o dil ki muraad dair mein hai na khaanqaah mein hai
'Hum kahan qismat azmaane jaayein' har sanam apni baargaah mein hai

Kaun aisa ghani hai jisse koi naqd-e shams-o qamar ki baat kare
Jisko shauq-e nabard ho humse jaaye taskheer-e kayanaat kare

~

32. Tere Gham Ko Jaan Ki Talaash Thi

Tere gham ko jaan ki talaash thi tere jaan nisaar chale gaye
Teri rah mein karte thhe sar talab sar-e raahguzaar chale gaye

Teri kaj adaai se haar ke shab-e intezaar chali gayi
Mere zabt-e haal se rooth kar mere ghamgusaar chale gaye
Na sawaal-e wasl na arz-e gham na hikaayatein na
    shikaayatein
Tere ahd mein dil-e zaar ke sabhi ikhtiyaar chale gaye
Yeh humin thhe jin ke libaas par sar-e raah siyaahi likhi gayi
Yahi daagh thhe jo saja ke hum sar-e bazm-e yaar chale gaye
Na raha junoon-e rukh-e wafa yeh rasan yeh daar karoge
    kya
Jinhein jurm-e ishq pe naaz tha woh gunahgaar chale gaye

~

33. Khatm Hui Baarish-e Sang

Naagahaan aaj mere taar-e nazar se kat kar
Tukde tukde huwe aafaaq pe khursheed-o qamar
Ab kisi simt andhera na ujaala hoga
Bujh gayi dil ki tarah raah-e wafa mere baad
Doston qaafila-e dard ka ab kya hoga
Ab koi aur kare parwarish-e gulshan-e gham
Doston khatm hui deeda-e tar ki shabnam
Tham gaya shor-e junoon khatm hui baarish-e sang

Khaak-e rah aaj liye hai lab-e dildaar ka rang
Ku-e jaanaan mein khula mere lahu ka parcham
Dekhiye dete hain kis kis ko sada mere baad
'Kaun hota hai harif-e mai-e mard afgan-e ishq'
Hai mukarrar lab-e saaqi pe sila mere baad

~

34. Rang Hai Dil Ka Mere

Tum na aaye thhe toh har ek cheez wahi thi ki jo hai
Aasmaan hadd-e nazar raahguzar raahguzar sheesha-e mai
    sheesha-e mai
Aur ab sheesha-e mai raahguzar rang-e falak
Rang hai dil ka mere 'khoon-e jigar hone tak'
Champayi rang kabhi raahat-e deedar ka rang
Surmayi rang ki hai sa'at-e bezaar ka rang
Zard patton ka khas-o khaar ka rang
Surkh phoolon ka dehekte huwe gulzaar ka rang
Zahr ka rang lahu rang shab-e taar ka rang
Aasmaan raahguzaar sheesha-e mai
Koi bheega hua daaman koi dukhti hui rag
Koi har lahza badalta hua aaina hai

Ab jo aaye ho toh thehro ki koi rang koi rut koi shai
Ek jagah par thehre
Phir se ik baar har ik cheez wahi ho ki jo hai
Aasmaan hadd-e nazar raahguzar raahguzar sheesha-e mai
    sheesha-e mai

~

35. Paas Raho

Tum mere paas raho
Mere qaatil mere dildaar mere paas raho
Jis ghadi raat chale
Aasmaanon ka lahu peeke siyah raat chale
Marham-e mushk liye nashtar-e almaas liye
Bain karti hui hansti hui gaati nikle
Dard ke kaasni paazeb bajaati nikle
Jis ghadi seenon mein doobe huwe dil
Aastinon mein nihaan haathon ki rah takne lagein
Aas liye
Aur bachchon ke bilakne ki tarah qulqul-e mai
Bahr-e naasoodagi machle toh manaaye na mane
Jab koi 'baat banaaye na bane'

Jab na koi baat chale
Jis ghadi raat chale
Jis ghadi maatami sunsaan siyah raat chale
Paas raho
Mere qaatil mere dildaar mere paas raho

~

36. Manzar (2)

Rahguzar saaye shajar manzil-o dar halqa-e baam
Baam par seena-e mehtaab khula aahista
Jis tarah khole koi band-e qaba aahista
Halqa-e baam tale saayon ka thehra hua neel
Neel ki jheel
Jheel mein chupke se taira kisi patte ka habaab
Ek pal taira chala phoot gaya aahista

Bahut aahista bahut halka khunuk rang-e sharaab
Mere sheeshe mein dhala aahista
Sheesha-o jaam suraahi tere haathon ke gulaab
Jis tarah door kisi khwaab ka naqsh
Aap hi aap bana aur mita aahista

Dil ne dohraaya koi harf-e wafa aahista
Tumne kaha
Aahista
Chaand ne jhuk-ke kaha
Aur zara aahista

~

37. Yahan Se Shahr Ko Dekho

Yahan se shahr ko dekho toh halqa dar halqa
Khinchi hai jel ki soorat har ek simt faseel
Har ek raahguzaar gardish-e aseeran hai
Na sang-e mil na manzil na mukhlisi ki sabeel

Jo koi tez chale rah toh puchhta hai khayaal
Ki tokne koi lalkaar kyun nahin aayi
Jo koi haath hilaaye toh wahm ko hai sawaal
Koi chhanak koi jhankaar kyun nahin aayi

Yahan se shahr ko dekho toh saari khalqat mein
Na koi saahib-e tamkeen na koi waali-e hosh

Har ek mard-e jawaan mujrim-e rasan ba-gulu
Har ik haseena-e rana kaneez-e halqa bagosh

Jo saaye door charaaghon ke gird larzaan hain
Na jaane mehfil-e gham hai ki bazm-e jaam-o sabu
Jo rang har dar-o deewar par pareshaan hain
Yahan se kuchh nahin khulta yeh phool hain ki lahu

~

38. Kis Harf Pe Tu-ne Gosha-e Lab Ay Jaan-e Jahaan Ghammaaz Kiya

Kis harf pe tu-ne gosha-e lab ay jaan-e jahaan ghammaaz
 kiya
Ailaan-e junoon dil waalon ne ab ke ba-hazaar andaaz kiya
Sau paikaan thhe paiwast-e gulu jab chhedi shauq ki
 lai humne
Sau teer taraazu thhe dil mein jab humne raqs aaghaaz
 kiya
Be-hirs-o hawa be-khauf-o khatar iss haath pe sar uss kaf
 pe jigar
Yun ku-e sanam mein waqt-e safar nazaara-e baam-e
 naaz kiya

Jis khaak mein mil kar khaak huwe woh surma-e chashm-e
  khalq bani
Jis khaar pe humne khoon chhidka hamrang-e gul-e
  tannaaz kiya
Lo wasl ki sa-at aa pahunchi phir hukm-e huzoori par humne
Aankhon ke dareeche band kiye aur seene ka dar baz kiya

~

39. Deewaar-e Shab Aur Aks-e Rukh-e Yaar Saamne

Deewaar-e shab aur aks-e rukh-e yaar saamne
Phir dil ke aaine se lahu phootne laga
Phir waz-e ihtiyaat se dhundla gayi nazar
Phir zabt-e aarzu se badan tootne laga

~

40. Kiye Aarzu Se Paimaan Jo Ma'al Tak Na
Pahunche

Kiye aarzu se paimaan jo ma'al tak na pahunche
Shab-o roz-e aashnaai mah-o saal tak na pahunche
Woh nazar baham na pahunchi ki muheet-e husn karte

Teri deed ke waseele khad-o khaal tak na pahunche
Wahi chashma-e baqa tha jisse sab saraab samjhe
Wahi khwaab motabar thhe jo khayaal tak na pahunche
Tera lutf vajh-e taskeen na qaraar sharh-e gham se
Ki hain dil mein woh gile bhi jo malaal tak na pahunche
Koi yaar jaan se guzra koi hosh se na guzra
Yeh nadeem-e yak-do saagar mere haal tak na pahunche
Chalo Faiz dil jalaayein karein phir se arz-e jaanan
Woh sukhan jo lab tak aaye par sawaal tak na pahunche

~

41. Dua

Aaiye haath uthaayein hum bhi
Hum jinhein rasm-e dua yaad nahin
Hum jinhein soz-e muhabbat ke siva
Koi bhut koi khuda yaad nahin

Aaiye arz guzaarein ki nigaar-e hasti
Zahr-e imroz mein sheereeni-e farda bhar de
Woh jinhein taab-e giraanbaari-e ayyaam nahin
Unki palkon pe shab-o roz ko halka kar de

Jinki aankhon ko rukh-e subh ka yaara bhi nahin
Unki raaton mein koi shama munawwar kar de
Jinke qadmon ko kisi rah ka sahaara bhi nahin
Unki nazron pe koi raah ujaagar kar de

Jinka deen pairvi-e kizb-o riya hai unko
Himmat-e kufr mile jurrat-e tahqeeq mile
Jinke sar muntazir-e tegh-e jafa hain unko
Dast-e qaatil ko jhatak dene ki taufeeq mile

Ishq ka sirr-e nihaan jaan tapan hai jisse
Aaj iqraar karein aur tapish mit jaaye
Harf-e haq dil mein khatakta hai jo kaante ki tarah
Aaj izhaar karein aur khalish mit jaaye

~

42. Sharh-e Bedardi-e Haalaat Na Hone Paayi

Sharh-e bedardi-e haalat na hone paayi
Ab ke bhi dil ki madaaraat na hone paayi
Phir wohi waada jo iqraar na banne paaya
Phir wahi baat jo isbaat na hone paayi

Phir woh parwaane jinhein izn-e shahaadat na mila
Phir woh shammein ki jinhein raat na hone paayi
Phir wahi jaan balabi lazzat-e mai se pehle
Phir woh mehfil jo kharabaat na hone paayi
Phir dum-e deed rahe chashm-o nazar deed talab
Phir shab-e wasl mulaqaat na hone paayi
Phir wahan baab-e asar jaaniye kab band hua
Phir yahan khatm munajaat na hone paayi
Faiz sar par jo har ik roz qayaamat guzri
Ek bhi roz-e makafaat na hone paayi

~

43. Jis Roz Qaza Aayegi

Kis tarah aayegi jis roz qaza aayegi
Shaayad iss tarah ki jis taur kabhi awwal-e shab
Be-talab pehle pahal marhamat-e bosa-e lab
Jisse khulne lagein har simt tilismaat ke dar
Aur kahin door se anjaan gulaabon ki bahaar
Yak ba yak seena-e mehtaab ko tadpaane lage

Shaayad iss tarah ki jis taur kabhi aakhir-e shab
Neem wa kaliyon se sarsabz seher

Yak ba yak hujra-e mehboob mein lehraane lage
Aur khamosh dareechon se ba-hangaam-e raheel
Jhanjhanaate huwe taaron ki sada aane lage

Kis tarah aayegi jis roz qaza aayegi
Shaayad iss tarah ki jis taur tah-e nok-e sinan
Koi rag waahima-e dard se chillaane lage
Aur qazzaaq-e sinaan-dast ka dhundla saaya
Az karaan ta ba karaan dahr pe mandlaane lage

Kis tarah aayegi jis roz qaza aayegi
Khwaah qaatil ki tarah aaye ki mehboob sifat
Dil se bas hogi yahi harf-e vida ki soorat
Lillaah-il hamd ba anjaam-e dil-e dil zadagaan
Kalma-e shukr ba naam-e lab-e sheereen dahnaan

~

44. Ashkabad Ki Ek Shaam

Jab sooraj ne jaate jaate
Ashkabad ke neele ufuq se
Apne sunehri jaam

Mein dhaali
Surkhi-e awwal-e shaam
Aur yeh jaam
Tumhaare saamne rakh kar
Tumse kiya kalaam
Kaha
Parnaam utho
Aur apne tan ki sej se uth kar
Ik sheereen paighaam
Sabt karo iss shaam
Kisi ke naam
Kinaar-e jaam
Shaayad tum yeh maan gayin aur tumne
Apne lab-e gulfaam
Kiye inaam
Kisi ke naam
Kinaar-e jaam
Ya shaayad
Tum apne tan ki sej pe saj kar
Thiin yun mahv-e aaraam
Ki raste takte takte
Bujh gayi shamm-e jaam

Ashkabad ke neele ufaq par
Ghaarat ho gayi shaam

~

45. Mere Dard Ko Jo Zubaan Mile

Mera dard naghma-e be-sada
Meri zaat zarra-e be-nishaan
Mere dard ko jo zubaan mile
Mujhe apna naam-o nishaan mile
Meri zaat ka jo nishaan mile
Mujhe raaz-e nazm-e jahaan mile
Jo mujhe yeh raaz-e nihaan mile
Meri khamoshi ko bayaan mile
Mujhe kayanaat ki sarwari
Mujhe daulat-e do jahaan mile

~

46. Ay Shaam Meherbaan Ho

Ay shaam meherbaan ho
Ay shaam-e shahr-e yaaraan

Hum pe meherbaan ho
Dozakhi dopahr sitam ki
Be-sabab sitam ki
Dopahr dard-o ghaiz-o gham ki
Be-zabaan dard-o ghaiz-o gham ki
Iss dozakhi dopahr ke taaziyaane
Aaj tan par dhanak ki soorat
Qaus dar qaus bat gaye hain
Zakhm sab khul gaye hain jinke
Daagh jaana tha chhut gaye hain
Tere toshe mein kuchh toh hoga
Marham-e dard ka doshaala
Tan ke uss ang par udha de
Dard sab se siva jahan ho
Ay shaam meherbaan ho
Ay shaam-e shahr-e yaaraan
Hum pe meherbaan ho
Dozakhi dasht nafraton ke
Bedard nafraton ke
Kirchiyaan deeda-e hasad ki
Khas-o khaashaak ranjishon ke
Itni sunsaan shahraahein
Itni gunjaan qatl gaahein

Jin se aaye hain hum guzar kar
Aabla ban ke har qadam par
Yun paon kat gaye hain
Raste simat gaye hain
Makhmalin apne baadalon ki
Aaj paon tale bichha de
Shaafi-e karb-e rahrawaan ho
Ay shaam meherbaan ho
Ay mah-e shab-e nigaaraan
Ay rafeeq-e dil-figaaraan
Iss shaam hum zubaan ho
Ay shaam meherbaan ho
Ay shaam meherbaan ho
Ay shaam-e shahr-e yaaraan
Hum pe meherbaan ho

~

47. Na Ab Raqeeb Na Naasih Na Ghamgusaar Koi

Na ab raqeeb na naasih na ghamgusaar koi
Tum aashna thhe toh thiin aashnaiyan kya kya
Juda thhe hum toh mayassar thiin qurbatein kitni

Baham huwe toh padi hain judaaiyaan kya kya
Pahunch ke dar pe tere kitne motabar thehre
Agarche raah mein huin jag hansaaiyaan kya kya
Hum aise sada dilon ki niyaaz mandi se
Buton ne ki hain jahaan mein khudaaiyaan kya kya
Sitam pe khush kabhi lutf-o karam se ranjeeda
Sikhaayin tumne hamein kaj adaaiyaan kya kya

~

48. Dhaka Se Waapsi Par

Hum ki thehre ajnabi itni madaaraaton ke baad
Phir banenge aashna kitni mulaqaaton ke baad
Kab nazar mein aayegi be-daagh sabze ki bahaar
Khoon ke dhabbe dhulenge kitni barsaaton ke baad
Thhe bahut bedard lamhe khatm-e dard-e ishq ke
Thiin bahut be-mehr subhein meherbaan raaton ke baad
Dil toh chaaha par shikast-e dil ne muhlat hi na di
Kuchh gile shikwe bhi kar lete munaajaaton ke baad
Unse jo kehne gaye thhe Faiz jaan sadqa kiye
Ankahi hi reh gayi woh baat sab baaton ke baad

~

184

49. Tum Apni Karni Kar Guzro

Ab kyun uss din ka zikr karo
Jab dil tukde ho jaayega
Aur saare gham mit jaayenge
Jo kuchh paaya kho jaayega
Jo mil na saka woh paayenge
Yeh din toh wohi pehla din hai
Jo pehla din tha chaahat ka
Hum jiski tamanna karte rahe
Aur jis se har dum darte rahe
Yeh din toh kitni baar aaya
Sau baar basse aur ujad gaye
Sau baar lute aur bhar paaya

Ab kyun uss din ki fikr karo
Jab dil tukde ho jaayega
Aur saare gham mit jaayenge
Tum khauf-o khatar se dar guzro
Jo hona hai so hona hai
Gar hansna hai toh hansna hai
Gar rona hai toh rona hai

Tum apni karni kar guzro
Jo hoga dekha jaayega

~

50. Kuchh Ishq Kiya Kuchh Kaam Kiya

Woh log bahut khush-qismat thhe
Jo ishq ko kaam samajhte thhe
Ya kaam se aashiqi karte thhe
Hum jeete ji masroof rahe
Kuchh ishq kiya kuchh kaam kiya
Kaam ishq ke aade aata raha
Aur ishq se kaam ulajhta raha
Phir aakhir tang aa kar humne
Donon ko adhoora chhod diya

~

51. Aaj Ek Harf Ko Phir Dhoondta
Phirta Hai Khayaal

(1)
Aaj ik harf ko phir dhoondta phirta hai khayaal

Madh bhara harf koi zahr bhara harf koi
Dil nasheen harf koi qahr bhara harf koi
Harf-e ulfat koi dildaar nazar ho jaise
Jisse milti hai nazar bosa-e lab ki soorat
Itna raushan ki sar-e mauja-e zar ho jaise
Sohbat-e yaar mein aaghaaz-e tarab ki soorat
Harf-e nafrat koi shamsheer-e ghazab ho jaise
Ta abad shahr-e sitam jisse tabaah ho jaayein
Itna taareek ki shamshaan ki shab ho jaise
Lab pe laaun toh mere hont siyah ho jaayein

(2)
Aaj har sur se har ik raag ka naata toota
Dhoondti phirti hai mutrib ko phir uski aawaz
Joshish-e dard se majnun ke garebaan ki tarah
Chaak dar chaak hua aaj har ik parda-e saaz
Aaj har mauj-e hawa se hai sawaali khalqat
La koi naghma koi saut teri umr daraaz
Nauha-e gham hi sahi shor-e shahaadat hi sahi
Soor-e mahshar hi sahi baang-e qayaamat hi sahi

~

52. Dil-e Mann Musaafir-e Mann

Mere dil mere musaafir
Hua phir se hukm saadir
Ki watan badar hon hum tum
Dein gali gali sadaein
Karein rukh nagar nagar ka
Ki suraagh koi paayein
Kisi yaar-e naama bar ka
Har ek ajnabi se poochhein
Jo pata tha apne ghar ka
Sar-e ku-e na-ashnaayaan
Humein din se raat karna
Kabhi isse baat karna
Kabhi usse baat karna
Tumhein kya kahun ki kya hai
'Shab-e gham buri bala hai'
Humein yeh bhi tha ghaneemat
Jo koi shumaar hota
'Humein kya bura tha marna
Agar ek baar hota'

~

53. Manzar (3)

Aasmaan aaj ik bahr-e pur shor hai
Jis mein har su rawaan baadalon ke jahaaz
Unke arshe pe kirnon ke mastool hain
Baadbaanon ke pehne huwe farghulein
Neel mein gumbadon ke jazeere kayi
Ek baazi mein masroof hai har koi
Abaabeel koi nahaati hui
Koi cheel ghote mein jaati hui
Koi taaqat nahin iss mein zor aazma
Koi beda nahin hai kisi mulk ka
Iski tah mein koi aabdozin nahin
Koi rocket nahin koi topein nahin
Yun toh saare anaasir hain yahan zor mein
Amn kitna hai iss bahr-e pur shor mein

~

54. Nazr-e Haafiz

Naaseham guft bajuz gham che hunar daarad ishq
Birau ay khwaaja-e aaqil hunare behtar azeen

(Haafiz)

Qand-e dahan kuchh isse zyaada
Lutf-e sukhan kuchh isse zyaada
Fasl-e khizaan mein lutf-e bahaaraan
Barg-e saman kuchh isse zyaada
Haal-e chaman par talkh-nawaayi
Murgh-e chaman kuchh isse zyaada
Dil shikani bhi dildaari bhi
Yaad-e watan kuchh isse zyaada
Shamm-e badan faanoos-e qaba mein
Khoobi-e tan kuchh isse zyaada
Ishq mein kya hai gham ke ilaawa
Khwaaja-e mann kuchh isse zyaada

~

55. Sitam Sikhlaayega Rasm-e Wafa Aise Nahin Hota

Sitam sikhlaayega rasm-e wafa aise nahin hota
Sanam dikhlaaenge raah-e khuda aise nahin hota
Gino sab hasratein jo khoon hui hain tan ke
    maqtal mein
Mere qaatil hisaab-e khoon baha aise nahin hota

Jahaan-e dil mein kaam aati hain tadbeerein na taazeerein
Yahan paimaan-e tasleem-o reza aise nahin hota
Har ik shab har ghadi guzre qayaamat yun toh hota hai
Magar har subh ho roz-e jaza aise nahin hota
Rawaan hai nabz-e dauraan gardishon mein
    aasmaan saare
Jo tum kehte ho sab kuchh ho chuka aise nahin hota

~

56. Hijr Ki Raakh Aur Wisaal Ke Phool

Aaj phir dard-o gham ke dhaage mein
Hum piro kar tere khayaal ke phool
Tark-e ulfat ke dasht se chun kar
Aashnaayi ke maah-o saal ke phool
Teri dehleez par saja aaye
Phir teri yaad par chadha aaye
Baandh kar aarzu ke palle mein
Hijr ki raakh aur wisaal ke phool

~

57. Nazr-e Maulana Hasrat Mohani

Mar jaayenge zaalim ki himaayat na karenge
Ahraar kabhi tark-e riwaayat na karenge
Kya kuchh na mila hai jo kabhi tujhse mile thhe
Ab tere na milne ki shikaayat na karenge
Shab beet gayi hai toh guzar jaayega din bhi
Har lehza jo guzri woh hikaayat na karenge
Yeh faqr-e dil-e zaar ka iwzaana bahut hai
Shaahi nahin maangenge wilaayat na karenge
Hum sheikh na leader na musaahib na sahaafi
Jo khud nahin karte woh hidaayat na karenge

~